Language Arts Idea Bank

Instructional strategies for supporting student learning

Graham Foster

Pembroke Publishers Limited

KH

*Dedicated to five educators
whose work has been
included in this book.*

*Sincere thanks to
Ken Bobrosky,
Mary Frampton,
Carl Horak,
Cathy Beveridge,
and
Viktoria Mustapic.*

© 2003 Pembroke Publishers
538 Hood Road
Markham, Ontario, Canada L3R 3K9
www.pembrokepublishers.com

Distributed in the U.S. by Stenhouse Publishers
477 Congress Street
Portland, ME 04101
www.stenhouse.com

We acknowledge the financial support of the Government of Canada through the Book Publishing Industry Development Program (BPIDP) for our publishing activities.

We acknowledge the Government of Ontario through the Ontario Media Development Corporation's Ontario Book Initiative.

National Library of Canada Cataloguing in Publication

Foster, Graham
    Language arts idea bank : instructional strategies for supporting student learning / Graham Foster.

Includes index.
ISBN 1-55138-158-3

1. English language—Study and teaching (Elementary)—Activity programs.
2. Language arts (Elementary) I. Title.

LB1576.F694 2003	372.6'044	C2003-903413-5

Editor: Kate Revington
Cover Design: John Zehethofer
Cover Photography: Ajay Photographics
Typesetting: Jay Tee Graphics Ltd.

Printed and bound in Canada
9 8 7 6 5 4 3 2 1

8/22/06

Contents

Introduction: Engaging Students in Language Arts

ACKNOWLEDGMENTS

The author gratefully acknowledges contributions of teachers from the Good Shepherd School, Okotoks, Alberta, and from Clear Water Academy, Calgary, Alberta.

Motivating students to learn, helping them focus well on their tasks, and nudging them to take ownership of their learning have always been challenges for teachers. They are, however, challenges that must be met.

Focused and motivated students typically learn effectively. With what seem to be increasingly rigorous program expectations, helping students become more actively engaged in their learning must be a priority. When students grow in their sense of personal responsibility, consideration of others, and independent know-how about completing tasks, teachers can experience the ultimate professional satisfaction.

Language Arts Idea Bank is intended to help teachers foster this growth in their students. It recognizes that students who fail to reach their potential usually do so because of ineffective strategies rather than lack of ability. Numerous viable strategies appear in this book, a collection of classroom-tested activities that have proven to help students learn more skillfully.

The activities have also assisted teachers in meeting classroom management challenges. Motivated and focused students tend not to disrupt the class. Therefore, while the book emphasizes motivation, it is mindful of the classroom management benefits of the idea bank entries.

Consistent with references to "text" in recent curriculum documents, *Language Arts Idea Bank* encompasses print, oral, and media texts. Critical thinking about text includes analyzing a host of oral language presentations as well as presentations in books, newspapers, magazines, radio, television, film, video and communication options available through computer technology. Most teachers recognize that range.

As might be expected from the book's title, the choice of teaching ideas highlighted here reflects personal preference and priority. The idea bank entries are rooted in personal professional challenges and issues raised by colleagues during more than 30 years in public education. Accompanied by familiar school scenarios, they are offered with the understanding that any pedagogical advice must be tempered to the reader's own classroom reality, needs, interests, and instructional style.

The language learning activities recommended in this book integrate reading, writing, speaking, listening, viewing and representing, as effective language learning activities typically do. For example, the representational activity of using a graphic organizer has been suggested in many variations towards the development of reading, writing, speaking, listening and viewing skills. The placement of each entry is based on the predominant language arts skill within it. Without doubt, though, placement has been a challenge.

More than 50 entries appear in the book, which is composed of four major parts based on language arts strands. The parts are as follows:

- A: Reading
- B: Writing
- C: Speaking and Listening
- D: Viewing and Representing

Typical of the dual emphasis on reading and writing in prescribed language arts programs, *Language Arts Idea Bank* offers more recommended activities for reading and writing than for the other language arts.

It is hoped that this book will prompt readers to engage in conversations with colleagues about their practice. Teachers wisely seek out suggestions related to their own professional assessments and concerns. Improving practice through ongoing professional conversations has frequently been described as the best professional development. Here, readers have the basis to develop their own language arts idea banks.

Part A   Reading

Part A offers idea bank entries related to wide-ranging reading skills and goals.

Reviewing Reading Strategies

These activities motivate students to think about themselves as readers and to consider the habits and strategies that will help them read with greater enjoyment and comprehension.

Promoting Close Attention to Text

These activities focus on a definite challenge for many students: thoughtfully attending to textual detail. Students who carefully attend to such detail improve their performance with a host of reading comprehension skills.

Responding to Reading

These activities invite students to connect text to their personal experiences, to recognize that reading can help them explore their personal worlds.

Exploring Vocabulary

These activities present interesting, productive alternatives to looking up words in a dictionary. In addition, the idea bank entries focus on having students learn and use important literary terminology.

Encouraging Frequent Reading

Research clearly indicates that frequent reading is directly linked to reading comprehension. These activities encourage students to read frequently for enjoyment. The final idea bank entry deals with censorship issues, an ongoing concern for Language Arts teachers.

- **Poetry with Passion** (page 35)
- **Assessing the School's Reading Program** (pages 36–37)
- **Dealing with Censorship Issues** (page 38)

Reading Profiles

At the beginning of the school year, you have students complete and file a reading profile. You wonder if this survey and other reading surveys might have more than "getting to know you" value.

Goal

To improve student understanding of the reading process through reading surveys.

How to Reach It

You could have students interview each other using a survey similar to the following at the start of the year. If you do so, schedule similar interviews three to ten times during the year. The interviewer and interview subject should use the survey to discuss what has changed, what has been learned, and what might be appropriate goals.

A variation would be for students to complete a survey on their own and to re-visit it three to ten times during the year. On each re-visit, students should note what has changed, what has been learned, and what might be appropriate goals. The survey that follows was completed by a Grade 6 student; a photocopiable version appears as an appendix.

Note: This survey could also be employed in a teacher-student conference.

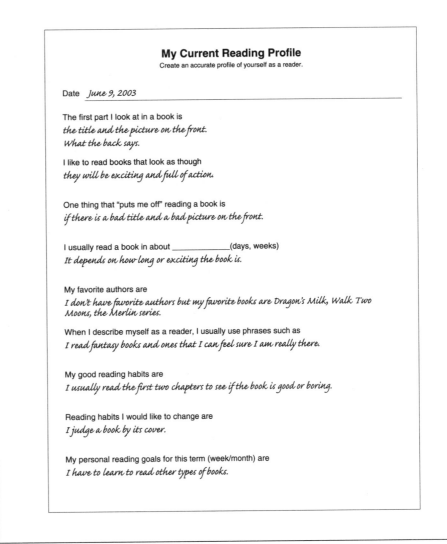

My Current Reading Profile

Create an accurate profile of yourself as a reader.

Date *June 9, 2003*

The first part I look at in a book is
the title and the picture on the front.
What the back says.

I like to read books that look as though
they will be exciting and full of action.

One thing that "puts me off" reading a book is
if there is a bad title and a bad picture on the front.

I usually read a book in about _____(days, weeks)
It depends on how long or exciting the book is.

My favorite authors are
I don't have favorite authors but my favorite books are Dragon's Milk, Walk Two Moons, the Merlin series.

When I describe myself as a reader, I usually use phrases such as
I read fantasy books and ones that I can feel sure I am really there.

My good reading habits are
I usually read the first two chapters to see if the book is good or boring.

Reading habits I would like to change are
I judge a book by its cover.

My personal reading goals for this term (week/month) are
I have to learn to read other types of books.

Helping Students Understand Themselves as Readers

Your students are stagnant in their reading skills. Top students earn top grades assignment after assignment; weak students remain weak.

Goal

To encourage students to improve reading skills by identifying personally effective reading strategies.

How to Reach It

Be sure to feature a host of instructional strategies related to the goal (see the before, during, and after strategies below) and to emphasize meta-cognition in your program. Metacognitive students are able to describe how they complete tasks and to identify their preferred options for getting things done. Students read better when they can identify specific strategies that will help them comprehend the text that they are reading.

You can help students become aware of themselves as readers by modelling and describing strategies, that is, the know-how or approaches used by effective readers, and by challenging students to identify strategies that work well for them personally. A practical approach is to have students employ a three-part framework to describe their strategies. They should ask themselves these questions:

1. What strategies do I prefer *before* I read this text?
2. What strategies do I prefer *as* I read this text?
3. What strategies do I prefer *after* I read this text?

The link between strategies and specific text reminds students that they may well employ different strategies to read a poem than they would use with an editorial.

Language arts professional literature frequently describes a viable reading process according to what effective readers often do before, during, and after reading. It's a good idea to adopt this terminology to describe reading strategies and to challenge your students to use similar terminology to describe the strategies that work best for them.

BEFORE READING

These strategies recognize that successful readers must fit what is in the text to what they already know about the subject of the text.

- Activating/building background knowledge: Someone familiar with curling, for example, will have the background to make sense of references to "hog lines," "hacks," "skip," "house," and "button"; someone unfamiliar with curling would benefit from building background knowledge to foster reading.
- Setting purpose: The purpose might be to gather information, to locate a specific fact, or to infer character traits. Setting purpose provides a focus for reading.
- Predicting or questioning: This activity also provides a focus for reading.

DURING READING

These strategies vary according to the text being read as well as the reader's preferences.

- Visualizing, or envisioning: This strategy refers to the benefit of picturing or "running the movie" in one's mind as one reads.
- Chunking text: Here, readers look for units of thought, such as sentences, stanzas, or paragraphs.
- Predicting and questioning: Effective readers often wonder what will follow in a text and express their wondering in a prediction or question. "I think that the butler did it." (Prediction) "Is someone other than the butler guilty?" (Question)
- Linking text to personal experience: This linking to personal experience is related to activating background knowledge. Personal experience of betrayal should help one understand and judge how well betrayal is presented in a novel.
- Monitoring for meaning: Effective readers respond to something that does not make sense to them by checking back in the text or checking a dictionary or other reference.
- Summarizing or paraphrasing: Putting a text in their own words allows effective readers to work out the essential meaning of the text.

AFTER READING

These strategies overlap with strategies at other stages in the process.

- Summarizing
- Checking predictions
- Answering questions
- Checking to refine interpretations: Successful readers do not settle on meaning too quickly; they interpret meaning and check the text to refine their interpretation. On multiple-choice reading tests, this strategy would take the form of checking the text before settling on one of the options for a question.

Some teachers have added an assessment of reading strategies to traditional assessment of reading comprehension. In addition to requiring students to answer questions about unfamiliar texts, teachers nudge students to note the strategies that they use before, during, and after the reading of the text. Through this approach, you can determine the extent to which students can describe and monitor their learning and processing, and you can emphasize the key point: Students who are able to describe their reading strategies are more skillful readers. The sheet that follows indicates how a Grade 6 student was encouraged to read metacognitively; a photocopiable version appears as an appendix.

Useful Reference

For further information about reading strategies and metacognition, see *I Think, Therefore I Learn!* by Graham Foster, Evelyn Sawicki, Hyacinth Schaeffer, and Victor Zelinski.

Understanding Myself as a Reader

Title of Text _____ *Pioneering by Lake Ontario by Catherine Traill* _____

Strategies I used before reading:

Before reading a story I look at the picture and make another picture in my mind that excites me.

Strategies I used during reading:

When I read I usually make pictures in my mind and picture myself being a character in the story. I also predict what will happen next and how the person feels.

Strategies I used after reading:

After reading I think of more content for the story or a better ending for the story.

My goals for future reading:

I want to read more adventurous books and I want to read longer, more exciting books.

What I have learned about myself as a reader:

I like to read people's lifelong story and how people have to survive. I also like books with exciting twists at the end.

The Unfolding Method to Improve Comprehension

Students demonstrate limited comprehension of text and cannot identify personally effective reading strategies.

Goal

To model a range of reading strategies.

How to Reach It

The "unfolding method" is one of many powerful approaches to foster awareness of personally effective reading strategies. The method works well with brief texts, especially shorter poems.

Direct the class to take out a piece of paper to cover selected text and to follow your directions to uncover the text, that is, to "unfold" it. The following sequence should work well.

Step 1. Have students uncover the title only and, if the text is illustrated, to examine the illustration. Ask what they think effective readers do before reading: they build or activate background knowledge, make predictions, and set a purpose for reading.

Step 2. Unfold a complete chunk of text, possibly a sentence or a paragraph. Ask why chunking helps readers. (Chunks, such as sentences, are complete thoughts or complete units). Ask students what they think effective readers do as they read. (They visualize, summarize, question, predict, and connect text to personal experience.)

Step 3. Focus on a selected strategy, such as visualization, questioning, predicting, or connecting. Ask students to share their ideas related to the selected strategy.

Step 4. Continue the unfolding process until the final chunk. Ask students to use their knowledge of the text to make a final prediction. Through this activity, students learn that the final chunk of a text often emphasizes the key point or may offer a surprising twist. In narratives, the final chunk often states or implies what is different for the protagonist or what has changed in the protagonist's life. When readers are uncertain about a text's meaning, they can often improve comprehension by focusing on the final chunk of the text.

Step 5. Ask students to write their interpretations, possibly by answering questions, and then to check the text to confirm and revise. Ask why this strategy is used by effective readers. (Effective readers refine interpretations and do not settle for an incomplete interpretation.)

A student's observations on an Eve Merriam poem, "The Stray Cat," follows; a photocopiable record sheet appears as an appendix.

Note: If students need to improve their habit of focusing on the text, complete the "unfolding method" as a written rather than as an oral exercise. Students could note responses on the blank sheet of paper as they follow the unfolding process.

Unfolding Method Record Sheet

Title _____ *"The Stray Cat" by Eve Merriam (poem)* _____

1. ILLUSTRATION AND TITLE UNCOVERED, TEXT COVERED
   My background knowledge, predictions, and reading purpose:
   Stray cats are friendly.

2. FIRST CHUNK OF TEXT UNCOVERED
   My visualization, paraphrase, question, or prediction:
   I think the family will take the cat in.

3. SECOND CHUNK OF TEXT UNCOVERED
   My visualization, paraphrase, question, or prediction:
   The poem will tell what the cat was like.

4. THIRD CHUNK OF TEXT UNCOVERED
   My visualization, paraphrase, question, or prediction:
   I was wrong before. The poem described what the cat was not like. Now it will tell what it was like.

5. FOURTH CHUNK OF TEXT UNCOVERED
   My visualization, paraphrase, question, or prediction:
   I predict that they will take the cat in.

6. FIFTH CHUNK OF TEXT UNCOVERED
   My visualization, paraphrase, question, or prediction:

   [The number of chunks varies with the size of the text.]

7. FINAL CHUNK OF TEXT UNCOVERED
   My interpretation, including answer, to my questions and judgment about my predictions:
   I was right but I didn't guess that they'd call the cat "Beauty."

Predicting Titles

Your students need toothpicks to keep their eyelids open when they are reading a text. You want them to learn strategies that help them focus on textual detail.

Goal

To focus on prediction as a useful reading strategy.

How to Reach It

Present brief texts to students, possibly samples of student writing; challenge students to predict the title that would fit the text. A variation is to have students read a brief piece of their own writing with the invitation for listeners to predict the title. While the exercises invite careful reading and listening, they also promote divergent thinking about possibilities. Students may well suggest plausible alternatives to titles selected by classmates and other authors. The following poems, by Grade 5 and 6 students, illustrate the method.

Actual Poem Titles: I —Vacant; II—A Dancer

Predicting Titles

I.   Title: _____

When darkness falls,
shadows sneak out
from hiding places.
They fly to the vacant lot
at the corner of our street.

As my eyes look out
through the window,
I see them creeping about.
I ask myself,
why oh why
do they come here?

Maybe to haunt me,
but why, I wonder.
What have I done?

Grade 6 Student

II.   Title: _____

Her legs hurt,
Her feet were sore,
But still,
She glided gracefully across the floor.

Her point shoes dirty,
Her legging torn,
But it was clear, a star was born.

Grade 5 Student

Sequencing Chunks of Text

You are concerned about students' reading comprehension. Comprehension suffers because students settle on meaning too quickly and do not attend to textual detail.

Goal

To encourage students to attend more carefully to the details in the text.

How to Reach It

Sequencing activities encourage close reading of text. An easy way to engage students in a sequencing activity is to cut up and scramble chunks of a brief text, possibly a newspaper article. Students determine the logical order of the chunks. Tactile learners would benefit if the chunks of the text were cut up so that they could be moved around when they are assembled. Obviously, such an approach demands more preparation time than the simple approach illustrated on the following page. The correct order of the chunks is D, B, E, A, and C.

Useful Reference

Enjoyable exercises that focus students on textual details can be found in *Precision Reading* by Ken Weber.

Princess Taller Following Surgery

Prince Andrew, son of Queen Elizabeth, revealed that his daughter, Princess Eugenie, grew by 5 cm during an operation to straighten her spine.

Before the seven-hour operation, the princess stood 160 cm tall. However, as of a few days later, she had grown by 5 cm. The prince expressed relief that Princess Eugenie's surgery corrected her scoliosis, a rare condition that affects one in 3000 people.

The princess's doctors indicated that the 5 cm increase in height is a typical result of the surgery. Scoliosis is a twisting of the vertebrae caused by an abnormal bending of the spine.

Following her recovery, the princess anticipates a normal, active life.

Sequence A to E

A   The princess's doctors indicated
that the 5 cm increase in height
is a typical result of the surgery.
Scoliosis is a twisting of the vertebrae
caused by an abnormal bending of the
spine.   _____

B   Prince Andrew, son of Queen Elizabeth,
revealed that his daughter, Princess Eugenie,
grew by 5 cm during an operation
to straighten her spine.   _____

C   Following her recovery, the princess
anticipates a normal, active life.   _____

D   Princess Taller
Following Surgery   _____

E   Before the seven-hour operation,
the princess stood 160 cm tall.
However, as of a few days later, she had grown
by 5 cm. The prince expressed relief
that Princess Eugenie's surgery corrected
her scoliosis, a condition that affects one
in 3000 people.   _____

Reconsidering Interpretations

You know that successful readers do not settle on meaning too quickly. Yet many of your students read through response assignments with the speed of midnight madness shoppers.

Goal

To encourage students to check text to confirm interpretations.

How to Reach It

Use a form similar to that completed by a Grade 5 student, below, to help students check and re-check text before they settle on meaning. Such a form can also allow students to learn from others in their exploration of texts. Note that students are invited to revise interpretations after careful rereading of text and class discussion. A photocopiable version of the form appears as an appendix.

This activity can be extended to a lesson on how to read tests effectively, including multiple-choice tests. Suggest that, once students have chosen an answer, they check the text again. For example, if a reading test requires students to define a word in line 15 of an accompanying text, students wisely check line 15 before they settle on their answer.

Reconsidering Interpretations

Title _____ *Horatius at the Bridge* _____

After my first reading, possibly the first part, chapter or section, I thought that
After reading the story I learned not to be afraid when tasks seem hard but stand up to them like Horatius did.

Is my understanding as complete and accurate as possible?
As I went on reading, I came to understand that
Horatius was also rewarded very well for his deed of saving the city.

After carefully rereading the text, especially those sections that I wondered about, I now understand that
Horatius was a real Roman soldier in the middle ages and that he was the strongest swimmer in Rome.

After discussing my understanding with others, I now think that
Horatius is like Eustace in The Silver Chair *because Eustace also took on a hard task without complaint.*

I am still not sure about

[The student did not have any uncertainties.]

The Reading Game

Students groan at yet another set of reading comprehension questions. A few ask the familiar "Do we have to?" question.

Goal

To engage students in a game that requires attention to textual detail and to thoughtful analysis of texts.

How to Reach It

An enjoyable activity for a moody Monday morning or a frosty Friday afternoon is to substitute the Reading Game for reading comprehension questions. The object of the game is to identify one of three student contestants who has heard a summary of a brief text, but has not read it. The other two student contestants have, of course, read the text. The rules are as follows:

1. Three students leave the room with two copies of a brief, unfamiliar text. Designate two of the students as readers. The third is not allowed to see the text, but is given an oral summary by the two readers and is allowed to ask questions. The two readers answer honestly.
2. The rest of the class reads the brief text and prepares questions designed to trap the non-reader. You may challenge students to include inferential and evaluative questions with their literal questions. Literal questions can be answered with information directly stated in the text. To answer inferential questions, readers must use background knowledge as well as textual detail. Evaluative questions call for an assessment of the effectiveness or value of the text. One of the best ways to attend to the details of a text—a challenge for many students—is to formulate appropriate questions.
3. When the three students return to the room, designated as Reader 1, Reader 2, and Reader 3, they honestly answer their classmates' questions to the best of their ability.
4. At the end of the game, the class votes on which of the three is the "non-reader."

To conclude the activity, challenge the three students to discuss what they have learned from the game. Typically, the three students indicate that, in future, they will be far more attentive to textual detail.

Hints:

- Start the game with three strong readers.
- The first time that you play the game, avoid designating the "non-reader" as Reader 1 since students often pose the first question to Reader 1. The non-reader often depends on or builds on a reader's answer (sometimes incorrectly).
- Designate three readers of similar reading ability as contestants in the game.

Page 21 shows one small group's choice of questions for student contestants.

The Reading Game

Group Three
Based on "Used" (see page 84)

FOR THE QUESTIONERS:

Questions About the Text:
Key literal question (Facts and information are in the text.)
What word does the writer use instead of thinking cap?

Key inferential question (Ideas are suggested, not directly stated.)
What was the girl's attitude toward the boy?

Key evaluative question (The reality and value of the text are judged.)
Why is the title effective?

Goals in formulating questions:
Ask more inferential questions.

FOR THE THREE CONTESTANTS:

What you learned from the activity:

Goals for future reading:

Connecting Literature to Personal Experiences

Some students in the class avoid reading because it does not seem to connect to their lives.

Goal

To emphasize writing and representational activities that connect text and personal experiences.

How to Reach It

"Extended Response to Reading," on page 23, and "My Personal Response to Literature," page 24, suggest possibilities to encourage students to connect literature with personal experience and to enter deeply the personal experience portrayed in the literary text. Many teachers have observed that writing based on personal connections to literature is often the most skillful writing that students produce and the strongest in voice.

Note: See "Benefiting from Oral Interpretation" under Part C, Speaking and Listening, for more on the readers' theatre option.

Useful References

For further information about a range of personal response options for students, see *Shared Reading in the Middle and High School Years* by Frank McTeague. For ideas related to selection of texts and engagement activities for reluctant readers, see *Reluctant Readers* by Ron Jobe and Mary Dayton-Sakari.

Extended Response to Reading

One of the most important reasons for reading is that it helps us think about our own lives. Some of the ways that we make connections between reading and our personal experiences are through writing, drawing, and dramatizing. The following suggestions will help you further explore connections you have already made through discussions or conferences. Consult with your teacher about other options.

- Write about an experience that you have had that is similar to an experience that you read about.
- Write about or draw a place to which you have been that is like a setting that you met in your reading. Focus on details that suggest your emotional response to the setting.
- Engage in role playing to illustrate a conflict similar to one you read about. Alternatively, you could write about such a conflict. Focus on showing your character's thoughts and feelings related to the conflict.
- Write about or sketch a familiar person similar to one you read about. The person could be from real life or from another text, such as a book or movie. Whether you are writing or illustrating, focus on the details that reveal the person's character.
- Write a series of diary entries for one of your characters. You might assume the role of the character. Capture your character's thoughts and feelings about various events.
- Re-write or perform a section of your reading in a different form. For instance, you might re-write or perform a story as a play.
- Write a sequel or an additional chapter, perhaps describing a character at a later stage of life.
- Write a diary entry from the perspective of a character at an earlier stage of life.
- Prepare and present an oral interpretation of the text or a brief oral report about a favorite author.
- Prepare and present a readers' theatre interpretation.
- In groups of three, prepare and present a scene in which you pretend to interview an author. One person assumes the role of the author; the other two act as the interviewers.

Suggestions

1. Considering RAFTS (Role, Audience, Format, Topic, Strong Verb/Purpose) will help you focus your assignment.
2. You can complete any of these assignments either individually or in small groups.
3. Conferences and revision activities will help you improve your work before you present it.

My Personal Response to Literature

Title   *"How Jadhu Became Himself" by Virginia Hamilton*

Personal response to literature includes our own thinking about and questioning of the text as well as connecting the text to our lives. In discussion with your teacher, decide on which of the following questions are appropriate to a text that you are interpreting.

1. a) What one question might you ask that would help you understand the text better?

   How does Jadhu change into all sorts of objects?

   b) What would be your most effective strategy for answering the question?

   Read the story again.

2. Identify what you consider to be the key passage of the text. Comment on why it is more appealing and more important than other passages.

   The key passage is where Jadhu learns to change into things. It is important because that is the whole point of the story.

3. Use the following frame to talk about something you learned from the text:
    At first I thought *that Jadhu was a poor man.*
    Later I realized that *he had magical powers.*

4. Identify recurrent patterns you noticed in the text. What might the author be emphasizing by the pattern?

   Jadhu not liking what he turns into is recurrent. He is emphasizing that Jadhu doesn't like to be animals, buildings, or machines.

5. a) Identify what you liked most and what you disliked most about the text.

   I liked most how Jadhu was eventually happy. I didn't like how Jadhu changed into things.

   b) What does your response reveal about your reading preferences?

   It tells me that I like fantasy stories.

6. a) Identify one page that you could reread so that you would better understand the text.

   I would reread page 198.

   b) To what extent did careful rereading affect your interpretation?

   It helped me understand how Jadhu changed into different objects.

Reading Logs as Alternatives to Book Reports

You know that research has clearly established the importance of frequent reading by students and that the amount of independent reading students do is positively related to reading comprehension. You build extensive reading into your program, but are looking for alternatives to book reports.

Goal

To introduce reading logs as an appropriate option for responding to text and possibly as an alternative to book reports.

How to Reach It

Set a minimum target of the number of books that students will read in the year, possibly one or two a month. Be sure to encourage parental cooperation in your efforts to foster reading. Think twice about establishing contests with prizes to promote reading. Many schools have discovered that with such contests the reading often ends with the contest. Your message must be that reading is its own reward, that it is often one's best entertainment option.

Nonetheless, there will be times when you want to confirm that the desired reading has taken place. In your promotion and documenting of reading, recognize the power of book talks. If you occasionally require students to present oral comments on books as an alternative to written reports, you will probably discover that reluctant readers will often accept a peer's recommendation of a good book.

Experienced teachers likely have file cabinets full of alternatives to book reports, including reading logs. In a reading log, students list books read and make a comment or representational response to each selection. They might set up a log as follows:

READING LOG

Name			Class
Title	Date Completed	Pages Read	Comments

Brief student-teacher conferences focused on reading logs can be scheduled throughout the year. Be sure to encourage students to share responses with classmates through book talks and general discussion.

What follows are samples of questions that invite students to respond to reading on their own terms:

- Would you like to read another book by the author? Why?
- What part of the text did you like the best?
- What surprised you most in your reading?
- What did your book help you to think about or understand?
- What other texts (including movies) are like this one? How?
- What would you change had you been the author?
- What does the book remind you of?
- What questions do you have about your novel?

Useful Reference

For further information about reading response options, see *Shared Reading in the Middle and High School Years*.

A Range of Responses to Free-Time Reading

Your class contains learners who prefer oral, visual, or dramatic responses to their reading. Others prefer to respond in a range of written forms. You decide to offer response options linked to learners' preferences.

Goal

To offer students a menu of structured response options for their personal free-time reading.

How to Reach It

"Options for Responding to Free-Time Reading" features possibilities for response. Obviously, the list could be extended. You might have students collect their responses in a section of their binders or in file folders. Don't forget about posting exemplars of exceptional student responses, making sure you follow the expected protocol for obtaining exemplars (see page 41). Through exemplars, you show students the quality of response that you are expecting.

Options for Responding to Free-Time Reading

1. Create a cover or poster for your title.
   Suggestion: Examine a variety of book covers before you design your own. Be prepared to discuss why your book cover suits the content of your book.
2. Create a shoebox collection of items that are important in your book.
   Suggestion: Challenge classmates to use your shoebox collection to guess the title of the book that you have represented.
3. Compose a headline and newspaper story for a major event in the novel.
   Suggestion: It is a good idea for you to examine models of newspaper stories before you write.
4. Prepare and present a talk-show interview about the book.
   Suggestions: You might work with another student who has read the book. One of you assumes the role of interviewer; the other, that of the author or a character. Consider presenting a videotaped version.
5. Compose a diary entry for your character.
   Suggestion: Ask your librarian to provide you with a published diary or a book written in diary form as a model.
6. Compose a monologue to illustrate a character's conflict.
   Suggestion: Ensure that your character's voice is clear, that the language is suitable to the character, and that the difficulty of the character's choice is evident.
7. Create a game or crossword.
   Suggestion: Consider using an actual game or crossword as a model.
8. Write a sequel chapter for your novel, possibly depicting events five or ten years later.
   Suggestion: Predict what might be different for characters in the future.
9. Write a letter intended for the author.
   Suggestion: In your letter, you might comment on your favorite character, your reaction to events and to the writer's voice, and your comments about the ending. Feel free to pose your questions about the text. (You don't necessarily have to send the letter.)
10. Compose a poem in response to the characters or events in your novel.
    Suggestion: When you write, focus on both your thoughts and emotions. In revisions, check that your word choice is precise and that your images are original.
11. Create a movie poster for your novel.
    Suggestion: Identify actors that you have chosen to portray the characters from your text.
12. Create a map or timeline for your novel.
    Suggestion: Try to locate books that include maps or timelines. Fantasy titles sometimes include maps.
13. Write an obituary for a character in your novel.
    Suggestion: Check the obituary section of a newspaper to review information typically contained in obituaries.
14. Dramatize a conflict in your novel.
    Suggestion: Remember that conflicts can be both external (a character against an outside force) and internal (a character against his own fears or doubts). For example, in Jack London's "To Build a Fire," the protagonist struggles against freezing weather (external conflict) as well as his own panic (internal conflict). Consider preparing a videotaped version of your dramatization.

Cumulative Responses to Text

You are seeking to encourage frequent reading by having students build on the responses of their classmates.

Goal

To motivate students to employ the responses of others to enhance students' understanding of a text.

How to Reach It

Develop a collection of file-folder responses to books read by students. The first reader of a given book indicates the title on a file-folder cover and inserts a written response. You might provide duplicated sheets with suggestions for personal responses in your file folders. A photocopiable version of one such sheet appears as an appendix. As the year proceeds, other readers contribute to the collection of responses, perhaps reacting to what other students have written. Usually, students should date and sign their responses. The following sample shows three responses by Grade 7 students.

Cumulative Responses to Text

Title   The Diary of Anne Frank   Author   *Anne Frank*

Once you have finished reading the book, write your response below. Feel free to respond to what classmates may have written about the book or respond to the book on your own terms. You might consider what you liked or disliked and why, what you wish had happened, what you thought of the characters, what the book reminded you of, your emotional reaction and your questions about the book/novel. **Be sure to date and sign your response.**

Response 1: I found this story interesting, yet moving. Some more immature students would have thought it disgusting. Personally I thought it was a truthful account of the feeling and thoughts of a teenage girl. For me it was very moving to read about the hardships of war. It was an account of much bravery. My opinion of the characters varies through the roughly two years in the secret annex. Anne started out as an immature, flighty teenager. She soon became serious and she contemplated her life. Most characters become much more mature. It was sad that many of the annexers lived a very short life.

Response 2: Anne Frank: The Diary of a Young Girl was an excellent account of the hardships of war, and the feelings of someone who was in the middle of it. It was very inspirational and moving, but at times it was slow and repetitive. The characters all go through dramatic changes that I think in some way helped them cope with the war. I agree with Rachael that it is a truthful account of the feelings of a young teenage girl during the war who showed a lot of bravery but in some places the story becomes slow and repeated a lot of unnecessary information which at times gets extremely boring. Overall, the story touched my heart, and helped me understand the hardships of war.

Response 3: Anne Frank: The Diary of a Young Girl was an amazing book. I agree with Julia and Rachael's statements in the sense that it is a truthful account, and was a very moving book. However, I disagree with the statement Rachael made, "Anne started as an immature, flighty teenager"; I think that Anne Frank was never what one would call immature. I found her to be an interesting person, and found ways in which I could relate to her. As she "matured," I found the book became increasingly dull. This was the only statement made by my classmates that I disagree with.

Is Looking Up Words in a Dictionary Always Necessary?

A steady diet of looking up words before one reads a text is unappetizing for most students. When you ask students to do so, once again you hear the "Do we have to?" response.

Goal

To encourage students to become engaged in learning new vocabulary.

How to Reach It

Two powerful instructional strategies—wordsplash and mapping—offer alternatives to that steady diet of looking up words in a dictionary.

Wordsplash stresses prediction of meaning as a pre-reading strategy. To achieve it, prepare a list of key words from a text or passage in an imaginative format; in other words, present some words angularly and vary the size of the words to represent meaning. Some of the words you select may be familiar to students, but may have a different meaning in context. For instance, many students may understand "work" to mean labor rather than an object or result of labor. After students read the text, have them check their predictions and note changed or modified understandings of the words. If students have no idea about the meaning of a word in the wordsplash, encourage thoughtful guessing. You may also choose to have students create their own wordsplash exercises.

The following wordsplash has been prepared for Roch Carrier's well-known story, "The Hockey Sweater."

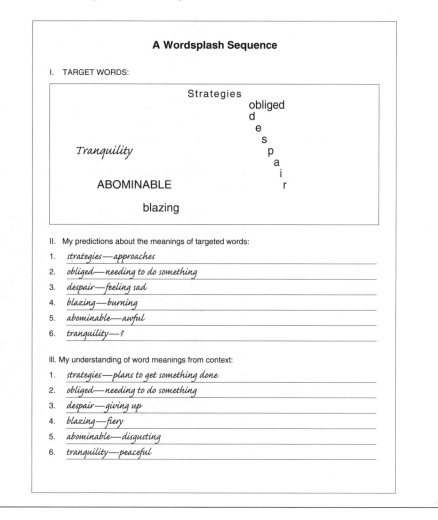

A Wordsplash Sequence

I. TARGET WORDS:

Strategies

obliged
d
e
s
p
a
i
r

Tranquility

ABOMINABLE

blazing

II. My predictions about the meanings of targeted words:
1. *strategies—approaches*
2. *obliged—needing to do something*
3. *despair—feeling sad*
4. *blazing—burning*
5. *abominable—awful*
6. *tranquility—?*

III. My understanding of word meanings from context:
1. *strategies—plans to get something done*
2. *obliged—needing to do something*
3. *despair—giving up*
4. *blazing—fiery*
5. *abominable—disgusting*
6. *tranquility—peaceful*

Mapping activities recognize that vocabulary instruction is most effective when students activate and extend their prior knowledge about a topic. A map such as the following tells students that learning new words is mostly about developing concepts and understandings.

Vocabulary Study

| Saying one thing; doing another | Offering a false response | Misleading a friend |

Characteristics

WORD
Hypocrisy

The opposite

honesty   genuineness

Examples
hypocrites

| Zulma's father in Harriet's Daughter | Mark's South African relatives in In Such a Place | The owner of Shiloh, the dog, in Shiloh |

The Character Graph Game

When studying literature, some students prefer unspecific descriptions of character traits such as "mad," "glad," "bad," and "sad" to precise, descriptive adjectives.

Goal

To motivate students to be precise in their descriptions of character traits.

How to Reach It

A representational activity focused on characterization is one method to add interest to character study. The activity can easily be turned into an instructional game.

Step 1. Explain to students that businesspeople frequently use graphs to represent various expenditures. For example, a pie graph is shown below.

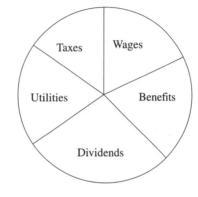

Step 2. Introduce the character trait graph to students by illustrating how pie graphs could be adapted to describe characters. Note that a character graph includes one clue to complement precise, descriptive character traits. Four is a good number of character traits to feature, but it's up to the students to determine an appropriate number of "slices."

Step 3. Let students infer the character whose traits have been represented in the graph. In the above example, the character is, of course, Tom Sawyer.

Essential Vocabulary for Analysis of Poetry

Both you and your students are put off by poetry anthologies with pages and pages of literary terminology.

Goal

To help students learn useful terminology to interpret poetry.

How to Reach It

Apply the fundamental rule that terminology is introduced only when it is related to the meaning of poems being read by students. The chart on page 33 attempts to focus on essential, not esoteric terminology. With meaning on the top line, it suggests that literary technique should always be linked to meaning. Promise students that you will not engage them in labelling exercises ("Underline three similes") divorced from meaning. It is also critical to establish that meaning is not the same as theme. Poems express ideas, but they also convey emotions or experiences. Discussion about a poem's meaning should include talk about emotions and experiences as well as ideas.

Meaning and Technique in Poetry

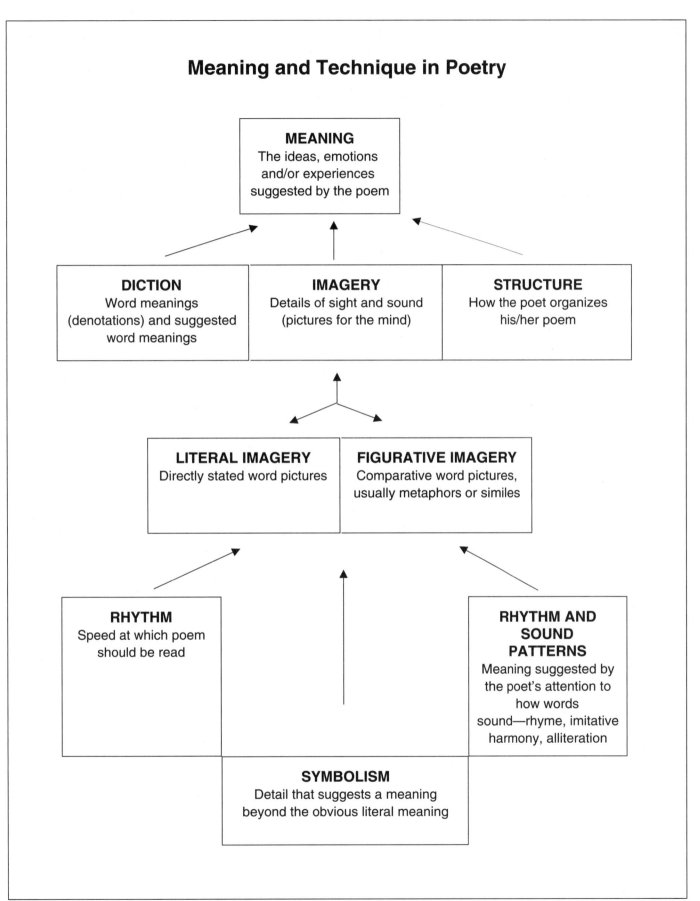

MEANING
The ideas, emotions and/or experiences suggested by the poem

DICTION
Word meanings (denotations) and suggested word meanings

IMAGERY
Details of sight and sound (pictures for the mind)

STRUCTURE
How the poet organizes his/her poem

LITERAL IMAGERY
Directly stated word pictures

FIGURATIVE IMAGERY
Comparative word pictures, usually metaphors or similes

RHYTHM
Speed at which poem should be read

RHYTHM AND SOUND PATTERNS
Meaning suggested by the poet's attention to how words sound—rhyme, imitative harmony, alliteration

SYMBOLISM
Detail that suggests a meaning beyond the obvious literal meaning

Sorting Out Literary Terminology

You have already decided that you will connect instruction in literary terminology to actual text that your students are studying. Now you are looking for an organizational strategy to use with literary terminology.

Goal

To motivate students to use context as well as a glossary to learn literary terminology.

How to Reach It

If your students use loose-leaf paper and binders, you might suggest that they establish a section entitled "Literary Terminology." Have them place several blank pages in the section: one page for each letter of the alphabet is recommended. As students learn about a literary term in the context of their instruction, they should note the definition in the glossary that they are creating. They should also note how the literary term is linked to meaning. For example, students might define conflict as a struggle between opposing forces whether these are people, natural forces, or ideas.

This glossary becomes useful when review is required. Students may add examples and refine definitions of literary terms as the school year proceeds. An enrichment option is for students to reorganize their glossary later in the year, possibly with the extension to a representational activity. You might ask students to include pictures to illustrate a targeted number of literary terms. These pictures can be drawn, downloaded from image banks, or clipped from magazines.

Poetry with Passion

Your students groan when you tell them that they will be studying poetry. Since you enjoy poetry and see it as significant in your life, you find these comments discouraging.

Goal

To encourage enjoyable and thoughtful reading of poetry by your students.

How to Reach It

Recommendation 1: Acknowledge that students may have different tastes in poetry than yours, but that most people enjoy some poetry. Working with poetry anthologies as well as core textual materials, invite all students to select one favorite poem. Set up a class schedule so that each student will orally present a favorite poem. (Guidelines for oral performance appear on page 91.) Following their performances, students comment briefly on the reason for their choices and invite brief comments and questions from classmates.

Recommendation 2: A second motivational strategy is to have students keep lists of catchy images and catchy wording as they read poetry. You can nudge them to understand that successful poets employ appropriate and unique images and pictures to communicate meaning.

Recommendation 3: Students could create their own anthologies: collections of a specified number of favorite poems complemented by brief comments about reasons for their choices.

Recommendation 4: Engage students in representational activities that allow them to illustrate poems, complemented with comments about how their illustrations emphasize important details in the text.

Assessing the School's Reading Program

You and your colleagues worry about the amount and the quality of reading done by students in your school. You want more of your students to say that they enjoy reading.

Goal

To cooperate with colleagues to assess the school's encouragement of frequent reading by students.

How to Reach It

The checklist on the following page may be an appropriate way to begin your collaborative action to encourage more frequent and thoughtful reading in your school. The checklist has been inspired by *Voices of Readers: How We Come to Love Books* by Robert Carlson and Anne Sherill. Each criterion is significantly related to your school's goal of increasing the amount of reading done by students.

Useful Reference

For a more comprehensive program assessment checklist, a checklist that includes criteria related to writing, listening, speaking, listening and viewing as well as reading, check *Standards for Learning* by Graham Foster. Program checklists are most effectively employed to decide on priorities for coordination at school rather than to simply pass judgment about the quality of the program.

A Checklist for Reflection About the School's Reading Program

_____ 1. My students have access to a wide collection of appealing books in the classroom and the library. The collection includes books-on-tape.

_____ 2. My students have the opportunity to hear texts read aloud.

_____ 3. My students have the opportunity to talk about favorite books and to listen to book talks from adults and from other students.

_____ 4. My students spend class time reading books of their own choosing.

_____ 5. My students are invited to select their own books for extensive reading.

_____ 6. My students read at least one novel or other book per month.

_____ 7. My students respond to their reading in a variety of ways or through response journals.

_____ 8. My students complete an intensive study of at least one book OR participate in mini-lessons related to reading they have chosen.

_____ 9. My students are encouraged to interpret sections of books on their own and to negotiate meaning with small groups of peers.

_____ 10. My students are encouraged to support their interpretations with specific and accurate references to the text.

_____ 11. My students are encouraged to note changes in their understanding of a book following discussion.

_____ 12. My students have been encouraged to use reading strategies such as visualizing, questioning, and checking when something doesn't make sense.

Dealing with Censorship Issues

You have decided to employ an Edgar Allan Poe story with your students. A parent calls to complain about your choice and to insist that you not use it with the class. You are upset by the call since you believe that the Poe story is an appropriate choice.

Goal

To communicate text selection procedures to parents and students.

How to Reach It

Few Language Arts teachers escape a censorship challenge during their careers. Since these can be extremely unpleasant, you are wise to inform yourself about your school district's policy related to public complaints about challenged materials. You are also wise to inform complaining parents about how your district handles such complaints and about their rights to influence your choice of content.

While many district policies indicate that no parent has the right to select learning resources for children other than their own children, you should offer an alternative to the child of the complaining parent whether or not this point appears in your district policy manual.

Remember that when you employ learning resources prescribed by your school district or educational authority such as the Ministry of Education, you can relay the complaint to the authority. When you choose resources that have not been authorized by legal authorities, you could be challenged. Therefore, you should always be ready to provide a specific and rational accounting for your selection.

Useful References

Books related to the important task of interpreting school programs to parents include *Standards for Learning*, *A Parent's Guide to Literacy for the 21st Century*, and *I Think, Therefore I Learn!*

Part B   Writing

Part B deals with current writing pedagogy with a focus on the challenge of helping students develop confidence as well as skill.

Using Rubrics and Exemplars

These activities focus on effective use of rubrics and exemplars—a current assessment emphasis, especially in the assessment of writing.

Revising and Rewriting

Recognizing that students often resist revision, these activities seek to motivate thoughtful revision of writing.

Strengthening Aspects of Writing

This sections targets specific technical matters, including vocabulary, poetry writing, spelling, usage, and organization.

Improving Expository Writing

Teachers have frequently observed that students would rather write narrative than expository text and that their narrative writing is more skillful than their expository writing. These activities focus on building students' confidence and competence as expository writers.

Developing a Viable Writing Process

These activities focus on students understanding themselves as writers and knowing the strategies and techniques that work best for them.

Finding a Voice

Voice has been described as the feature that separates exceptional writing from competent writing. These activities aim to help students discover and refine their voice as writers.

Learning Through Rubrics and Exemplars

Students demonstrate uncertainty about the requirements of an assignment. They are not sure what to do and how to proceed.

Goal

To encourage students to be more attentive to the requirements of a writing assignment and the options for completing it.

How to Reach It

Recommendation 1: For a specific writing assignment build a simple rubric with your students. A four-point rubric can be designed to describe levels of performance: 1. Weak; 2. Novice; 3. Competent; 4. Proficient. Begin by describing the major categories to be assessed, for example, Content, Organization, Sentence Structure, Vocabulary, and Conventions as a group of junior high teachers chose for their rubric for expository writing (page 42). The challenge, of course, is to differentiate specific graduations of quality among the selected categories. For example, what separates a proficient from a competent performance?

Recommendation 2: An alternative is to engage students in modifying a rubric, possibly selected from a teacher's guide, a Web site, a colleague, or a commercial source. In reflecting on the assignment, students are invited to add, delete, or modify criteria on the rubric so that the rubric is a closer fit to the specific assignment.

Recommendation 3: Another powerful approach is to work backwards from exemplars to rubrics. Show students samples of work completed by other students in response to a similar task. The exemplar need not be a print sample; it may be a poster, an audiotape or a videotape, depending on the task. Begin to collect student work for use with other classes in subsequent years. It is wise to present exemplars anonymously and to request parental permission for use of those you collect. Your own version of the request form below should serve you well, especially if your District requires parental permission to collect exemplars.

Dear _____:

I would very much like to employ the enclosed work sample completed by your child as an instructional resource with other classes. Such samples are useful in instructing students about important program expectations.

Current District expectations require parental approval for use of a student's work as a learning resource. If you are agreeable to this use, please sign the attached permission form.

I have already received your child's permission to use the work sample to help other students learn. Please be assured that your child's work will be presented anonymously and that it will always be honored as an instructional resource.

If you have any question or concerns, please call me at _____.

Sincerely,

....

PERMISSION FORM

Date _____

I grant permission for _____ School to employ the work of my child, _____, as an instructional resource to be presented anonymously. The work is entitled "_____."

_____

Parent's signature

Expository Writing Rubric

	Level 4 Proficient	Level 3 Competent	Level 2 Novice	Level 1 Weak
CONTENT	-Consistently uses thoughtful and insightful ideas related to purpose -Consistently employs ideas relevant to the topic -Clearly offers a complete preview	-Regularly uses thoughtful and insightful ideas related to purpose -Regularly employs ideas relevant to the topic -Offers a preview	-Sometimes uses thoughtful and insightful ideas related to purpose -Sometimes employs ideas relevant to the topic -Offers a partial preview	-Rarely uses thoughtful and insightful ideas related to purpose -Rarely employs ideas relevant to the topic -Offers little evidence of a preview
ORGANIZATION	-Uses unique beginning that hooks the reader -Consistently employs a topic sentence to begin paragraphs -Consistently employs effective transitions among paragraphs	-Uses interesting beginning that hooks the reader -Regularly employs a topic sentence to begin paragraphs -Regularly employs effective transitions among paragraphs	-Attempts interesting beginning that hooks the reader -Sometimes employs a topic sentence to begin paragraphs -Sometimes employs effective transitions among paragraphs	-No attempt to capture attention -Seldom employs a topic sentence to begin paragraphs -Rarely employs effective transitions among paragraphs
SENTENCE STRUCTURE	-Demonstrates effective and appropriate sentence lengths -Demonstrates unique and varied use of sentence openers	-Demonstrates varied sentence lengths -Demonstrates varied use of sentence openers	-Demonstrates little variety in sentence lengths -Demonstrates little variety in use of sentence openers	-Demonstrates no variety in sentence length -Demonstrates no variety in use of sentence openers
VOCABULARY	-Chooses words that are consistently precise and appropriate for the audience -Frequently chooses unique and creative words	-Chooses words that are precise and appropriate for the audience -Occasionally chooses unique and creative words	-Chooses words that are sometimes precise and appropriate for the audience -Begins to choose unique and creative words	-Chooses words that are seldom precise and appropriate for the audience -Makes limited choices in regard to creative words
CONVENTIONS	-Always maintains appropriate tense usage -Always uses correct punctuation -Always uses correct spelling of high frequency words and words important in unit of study -Consistently avoids run-on sentences	-Regularly maintains appropriate tense usage -Regularly uses correct punctuation -Regularly uses correct spelling of high frequency words and words important in unit of study -Regularly avoids run-on sentences	-Sometimes maintains appropriate tense usage -Sometimes uses correct punctuation -Sometimes uses correct spelling of high frequency words and words important in unit of study -Sometimes avoids run-on sentences	-Rarely maintains appropriate tense usage -Rarely uses correct punctuation -Rarely uses correct spelling of high frequency words and words important in unit of study -Rarely avoids run-on sentences

Imaginative Exemplars Please!

You observe that teachers' guides for recently authorized resources are replete with rubrics. Some are very useful for instruction and assessment; however, students are often foggy about the meaning of criteria in rubrics.

Goal

To improve student work with rubrics through complementary work with exemplars.

How to Reach It

Exemplars, or samples of student work for a task, show what is expected; rubrics merely tell. Over the past few years, many teachers have observed that exemplars are necessary complements to rubrics. Students work more effectively with rubrics when they have first worked with corresponding exemplars. You are wise to collect samples of student work for instruction with future classes.

The following exemplars have been designed to do more than present samples of effective work. Note that two versions of each piece are used with a class—the student writer's original work and a modified version. Students use the modified version to think about the writer's options before they check the original text. This technique motivates more careful attention to the exemplars than would occur if the teacher simply presented an example of effective work.

For the "White Water Adventure" exemplar, note that in Version A words have been omitted (1a and 1b); students use context to consider appropriate, evocative possibilities. Two chunks of text (2a and 2b) contain nothing but simple sentences beginning with a subject. Students combine the simple sentences to create complex sentences. The large blank at the conclusion of the story challenges students to consider an effective ending—one that offers a surprising twist or an indication of what the protagonist has learned or what has changed.

"The Smelly Box" models another possibility for the imaginative use of exemplars. Version A is a degraded text of the student writer's original text, Version B. Students are challenged to compare and contrast the two pieces to determine which is superior. Students employ the number codes to make specific comparisons:

1. Students compare endings.
2. Students determine which exemplar is superior in showing rather than telling.
3. Students compare sentence patterns.
4. Students consider vocabulary choices.

Obviously, in working with these and other exemplars, students could be invited to attend to many other specific features, such as story structure—possibly conflict, climax and resolution—or conventions—possibly punctuation, especially quotation marks.

A critical final step in work with exemplars involves students revising their own writing with the specific criteria explored through the exemplars.

White Water Adventure

Version A

"Dad! It's too high!"

But my voice drowned in the **1a**_____sound of the enormous rapids. Straining, I forced myself to paddle to reach my destination safely. The paddles seemed to be **1b**_____by the power of the mighty waves.

I looked back at my dad with pleading eyes, but only saw a frustrated figure paddling vigorously trying to steer the kayak to safety. My face was frozen with fear; I was out of control. The kayak collided with an enormous boulder, plunging my father and me into the icy, cold water. I heard the threatening roar of the waves as they rocketed against the barren cliff face. **2a** (I felt myself being hurled under the overpowering waves. I gasped for air. My body swayed helplessly in the waves.) **2b** (My head crashed into a boulder. I fell unconscious.)

I woke. I was in a daze. I saw a blurred figure of my father standing over me. My dad carried me to our car. _____

_____.

Grade 6 Student

White Water Adventure

Version B

"Dad! It's too high!"

But my voice drowned in the thrashing sound of the enormous rapids. Straining, I forced myself to paddle to reach my destination safely. The paddles seemed to be hypnotized by the power of the mighty waves.

I looked back at my dad with pleading eyes, but only saw a frustrated figure paddling vigorously trying to steer the kayak to safety. My face was frozen with fear; I was out of control. The kayak collided with an enormous boulder, plunging my father and me into the icy, cold water. I heard the threatening roar of the waves as they rocketed against the barren cliff face. I gasped for air. As I felt myself being hurled under the overpowering waves, my body swayed helplessly. Crashing into a boulder, I fell unconscious.

I woke. I was in a daze. I saw a blurred figure of my father standing over me. My dad carried me to our car. Groggily, I mumbled, "I told you it was too high!"

Grade 6 Student

The Smelly Box
Version A

Mr. Thorkild was Sue and Tim Johnson's new neighbor. On a moonlit night they saw him burying a box in his yard.

2 <u>Sue walked over to her brother and said, "I wonder what could be in the box?"</u>

"Never you mind, Silly, it's none of our business," Tom answered with an indifferent laugh.

"But as Canadian citizens it's our business to know what's going on in our neighborhood," Sue protested.

"It is?" Tim paused, then continued: "Even if it is, we're only eleven and twelve, whom would you believe—two crazy kids or a full grown middle-aged man?"

4 "I guess you have a point," Sue <u>said in response.</u>

4 They finally drifted off into a <u>deep</u> sleep.

The following afternoon when the twosome arrived back home after school, Sue was still mystified by the box. Tim swore to himself he would not let his little sister's feeble tries to help her solve the mystery affect him. It turned out that he was the feeble one. Before he knew it, he was being practically dragged to Mr. Thorkild's front steps. They had decided, or rather Sue had decided, that Tim would just plainly ask him, "What is in the box?"

3 <u>They asked him. He simply stated,</u> "Why it's just some rotted old meat. It was stinking up the house. Why don't you come in and tell me what raised your suspicions. I can set up some cookies and milk for you two."

"We'd love it."

"Yeah right, like she said, we'd love to but mom wants us to get going home. B-B-Bye." Tom stuttered for he was quite embarrassed.

3 <u>Then they walked up the steps of their home. Sue suddenly stopped in her tracks and said, "Hey, he never let us see inside the box. He could be telling us stories!"</u>

1 "I hope he isn't," he replied.

Grade 5 Student

The Smelly Box
Version B

Mr. Thorkild was Sue and Tim Johnson's new neighbor. On a moonlit night they saw him burying a box in his yard.

2 <u>Sue shivered and in a quivering voice said, "I wonder what could be in the box?"</u>

"Never you mind, Silly, it's none of our business," Tom answered with an indifferent laugh.

"But as Canadian citizens it's our business to know what's going on in our neighborhood," Sue protested.

"It is?" Tim paused, then continued: "Even if it is, we're only eleven and twelve, whom would you believe—two crazy kids or a full grown middle-aged man?"

4 "I guess you have a point," Sue <u>replied glumly.</u>

4 They finally drifted off into a <u>troubled</u> sleep.

The following afternoon when the twosome arrived back home after school, Sue was still mystified by the box. Tim swore to himself he would not let his little sister's feeble tries to help her solve the mystery affect him. It turned out that he was the feeble one. Before he knew it, he was being practically dragged to Mr. Thorkild's front steps. They had decided, or rather Sue had decided, that Tim would just plainly ask him, "What is in the box?"

3 <u>After they asked him, he simply stated,</u> "Why it's just some rotted old meat. It was stinking up the house. Why don't you come in and tell me what raised your suspicions. I can set up some cookies and milk for you two."

"We'd love it."

"Yeah right, like she said, we'd love to but mom wants us to get going home. B-B-Bye." Tom stuttered for he was quite embarrassed.

3 <u>As they walked up the steps of their home, Sue suddenly stopped in her tracks and exclaimed, "Hey, he never let us see inside the box. He could be telling us stories!"</u>

1 "Here we go again," he whispered with a defeated sigh.

Grade 5 Student

Marking Strategy for Writing

You spend hours marking student assignments, especially writing assignments. Although you often write detailed comments and suggestions, you are frustrated because many students do not heed your advice on subsequent assignments. Once some students have asked the "What did ya' get?" question about their marks, they pay attention to little else.

Goal

To adopt a marking strategy that is more effective in improving subsequent writing completed by your students.

How to Reach It

Begin by clarifying with students that when you read their assignments, you wear two hats: those of assessor and instructor. You want to know how well students have performed with targeted skills; more than that, you want them to learn from the assignment so that they perform better on subsequent assignments.

Be consistent in employing the following assessment strategy:

- Write or offer a single suggestion based on the most fundamental need. In offering too many suggestions, you draw attention to none.
- Write or offer one positive comment, if possible. Notice and praise a positive feature to affirm your students.
- Engage students in keeping a "Goals" and "Goals Achieved" record related to your assessment. Related to this point, nudge students to use one or two of these goals as revision criteria in subsequent assignments.
- Use a specific marking scale or rubric for purposes of accountability.

The form on page 48 serves as one vehicle for constructive assessment.

Useful Reference

Kathy Paterson's *Help! Survival Strategies for Teachers* contains guidelines for the assessment of student writing.

Marking Form

Student Name _____

Assignment _____

POSITIVE FEATURES

I am most impressed with

SUGGESTION

I believe that your priority for improvement is

RUBRIC OR MARKING FORM ATTACHED   Yes ❑   No ❑

Revision Game

In your less diplomatic moments, you refer to your lively class as being "off the wall." You are facing another one of those moody Monday mornings or frosty Friday afternoons. You seek engaging activities to help students learn about effective writing techniques.

Goal

To motivate students to learn about effective writing techniques through a game.

How to Reach It

Have your students apply selected criteria from the following page to a literary text or to an exemplar of effective student writing. As they make detrimental changes to an effective example, students will come to learn more about writing techniques, including the labelling of effective techniques. The interest of unmotivated students may quicken in picking out effective examples when they assume the "spoiler" role.

Note: Some classes require a friendly reminder that profane changes are unacceptable.

Following the exercise, encourage students to return to serious revision by reviewing a piece of their own writing to apply the criteria they have been learning about.

Playful Exploration of Exemplars or Literary Texts

CONTENT

- Find a place in the text where you will add one point that may be fascinating, but clearly distracts from the author's purpose.

- Find a place in the text where you will delete one point that will be clearly detrimental to the author's purpose.

ORGANIZATION

- Consider how the movement of one paragraph or chunk of text would damage the composition. Describe the movement of a paragraph or chunk of text that would harm the flow of writing.

SENTENCE STRUCTURE

- Rewrite one paragraph with nothing but simple sentences. Is your revision helpful or hurtful? Why?

VOCABULARY

- Copy a sentence that has descriptive vocabulary. Rewrite the sentence so that the words are dull and ordinary.

CONVENTIONS

- Copy three sentences that are free of errors. Rewrite the sentences to illustrate that an error in grammar/usage confuses the reader. Which distracting usage error should you correct in your own writing?

Revision with Gusto

Students fail to revise written assignments carefully.

Goal

To focus your students on specific criteria for the revision of writing.

How to Reach It

One reason that students fail to revise carefully is that they lack specific revision criteria. "Read each others' papers and make suggestions" is too general for many students. Be sure that students are aware of the specific criteria for the assignments.

For example:

- My argument is clearly stated.
- My reasons contain specific facts and details.
- Each of my paragraphs focuses on a specific topic.
- I have checked that there is variety in sentence structure, in other words, that not all of my sentences begin with a subject.

When students work individually or with a partner, encourage them to use an imaginative revision strategy. Two options are particularly useful:

- Have students write specific criteria on Post-it notes and draw an arrow in pencil from the Post-it note to the section of the text that demonstrates the desired feature. (See below.)
- Allow students to revise with the help of highlighters—a different color for each criterion. Obviously, the class must use consistent color coding for the strategy to work.

The Post-it note and color-coding strategies work best with a limited number of criteria—four to six.

Useful Reference

Specific criteria related to a variety of writing forms can be found in *Student Self-Assessment*.

An Illustration of Post-it Note Criteria Strategy

Detail that best conveys mood → The moisture-deprived fall air evaporated the perspiration on my windswept face, as I raced headlong down the dusty gravel path. Despite the dilapidated condition of the bike on which I sat, I still hugged corners, like a hovercraft skinning the breakers, ← Colorful word choice with a rush of adrenaline, a rush that could be provided by few other activities. As the dead leaves became even deader with a crunch, crinkle, snap and I rocketed further down the twisted abyss of speed and motion, my overworked heart pulsated more laboriously. An unavoidable weariness began to hang over me, like a dark storm cloud, heavy with thunder. My aching ← Effective metaphor or simile hamstrings, and overheated body were not what they were five minutes ago … had it been five minutes? It seemed like centuries. So I hopped off my bike, and wondered why I had been compelled to get on in the first place.

Grade 9 Student

Goal Setting for Personal Errors

Students repeat errors or weaknesses from previous writing assignments or reports. You are frustrated that the hours you spend marking compositions yield limited improvement in subsequent writing.

Goal

To encourage students to work independently to meet personal writing needs.

How to Reach It

Recommendation 1: Throughout the year, have students keep a goals chart similar to the one outlined below. For younger students, the headings could be "Can Do" and "Need to Do." The chart nudges students to identify their personal learning challenges and to celebrate the achievement of learning outcomes.

MY PERSONAL WRITING GOALS

Goals	Goals Achieved

Recommendation 2: A related strategy is for students to identify a personal revision criterion for every assignment—a criterion taken from their goals list. If students employ the Post-it note or highlighter revision strategy, discussed in the previous scenario, one Post-it note or one color could be devoted to the student's individual goal.

Useful Reference

A student-friendly handbook for grammar and usage is *The Grammar Handbook for Word-wise Kids* by Gordon Winch and Gregory Blaxell.

To Be or Not to Be; To Have and Have Not

Your students employ much colorless vocabulary in their writing.

Goal

To motivate students to be precise and colorful in their choice of verbs.

How to Reach It

Have students select a piece of their own writing. Following a review of past, present, and future tense forms of "to be," ask them to write a section, possibly one or two paragraphs, replacing all forms of the verb "to be." Examples:

> Sunlight spread across the city.
> Not: It was a sunny day.
> Clara, the protagonist of the story, faces an identity crisis.
> Not: Clara is the protagonist of the story.

You can also encourage students to explore alternatives for all forms of **to have**, **to go**, and **to get**. Students could use a form such as that shown filled in below to record the before-and-after versions of some sentences.

Useful Reference

A range of instructional strategies focused on important elements of writing, including vocabulary, can be found in *Student Self-Assessment*.

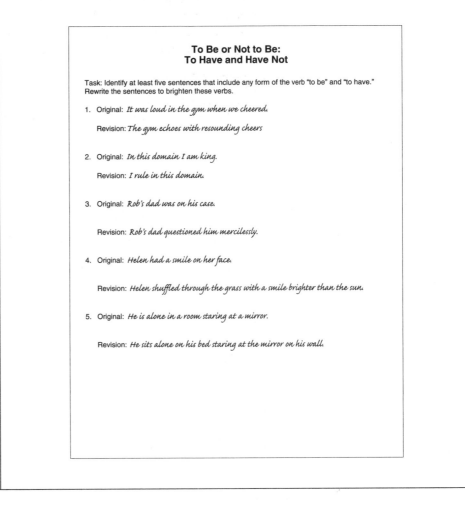

To Be or Not to Be:
To Have and Have Not

Task: Identify at least five sentences that include any form of the verb "to be" and "to have." Rewrite the sentences to brighten these verbs.

1. Original: *It was loud in the gym when we cheered.*

   Revision: *The gym echoes with resounding cheers*

2. Original: *In this domain I am king.*

   Revision: *I rule in this domain.*

3. Original: *Rob's dad was on his case.*

   Revision: *Rob's dad questioned him mercilessly.*

4. Original: *Helen had a smile on her face.*

   Revision: *Helen shuffled through the grass with a smile brighter than the sun.*

5. Original: *He is alone in a room staring at a mirror.*

   Revision: *He sits alone on his bed staring at the mirror on his wall.*

Showing, Not Telling

Your students' writing tells rather than shows. Student writers are much more likely to write "Nancy was mad" than "Nancy stormed into the room, grabbed the telephone and smashed it into the wall."

Goal

To focus students on showing rather than telling in their writing.

How to Reach It

To help students learn about showing rather than telling, employ an exemplar such as that on the following page. An alternative is to use a text that students are studying, possibly one from a literature anthology.

Have students place a "T" over sentences that mostly tell and an "S" over sentences that mostly show. After they finish the exercise, challenge students to revise a piece of their own writing, using Post-it notes or a highlighter to illustrate effective showing rather than telling.

Showing, Not Telling

Place a "T" over sentences that tell and an "S" over sentences that show.

The House on the Hill

It was dark already! Shelly, Cindy and I had stayed at the library too long. We decided to take the short cut home because if we went the other way, it would be even darker before we got home. We would have to go past the house on the hill but we were not afraid.

We walked quickly for about five minutes. Suddenly, we heard whispering. It came from behind us. Turning around, we expected to see someone, but it was too dark. We hurried on, our hearts beating rapidly. As we walked along a white picket fence, an animal suddenly howled! The sound frightened us.

We could hear whispering again and another howl. I got goose bumps! It sounded too close for comfort. A door creaked in the distance and a man laughed like a hyena. This time we ran! Shelly reminded me of the house that we had passed. I really did not think it was haunted, but I thought so now!

Cindy screamed!

In the moonlight, a tall figure was coming towards us. It did not have a head! I walked kind of jerky. I could not move! All of a sudden my big brother came rushing up on his bike. He zoomed up to the headless man and knocked him down! We were surprised to see Bobby on stilts!

Out of the bushes came Tommy and Joey. They played a trick on us! I'm glad my brother was worried about me and came to look for me! Now he's going to help us plan a good way to scare those boys back!!!!!

Grade 5 Student

Vocabulary Challenge

Your students' writing reflects too much vague, unspecific word choice.

Goal

To focus students on the importance of strong specific word choices in their writing.

How to Reach It

Step 1. Write the following brief poem on the board.

> The rain is like
>
> *small*
>
> *silent*
>
> *strangling*
>
> *hands.*

Close by, rewrite the poem substituting the following words for those in italics: "petite," "quiet," "constricting," and "appendages." You may also wish to invite students to provide some alternatives. Discuss how the substitutions affect the tone and impact of the poem. Emphasize the need for strong, deliberate word choices in order to maximize the effect of writing.

Step 2. In order to enhance descriptive writing, many writers pay particular attention to adjectives. Discuss how using a long string of adjectives may not be as effective as using one strong descriptor. Note also that a connotative adjective often sets the tone for a scene. For example, if a girl felt particularly uncomfortable in front of someone whom she had once liked and now intensely disliked, you might write: *June stared at the rough, gray, concrete floor.* However, to capture the mood of the scene, a better description might simply be: *June stared at the cold floor.*

Discuss how overly used adjectives are often too vague to be effective, by using the following examples to define the word "nice."

- My father is so nice: he gives me money whenever I ask for it.
- Tara looks so nice today. I just love her hair that way.
- Whenever Fritz growls, I say "Nice dog," and he stops.
- Mrs. Nelson is the nicest old lady. She gives us cookies on the way home from school.
- "Hey Mom, the class voted me most likely to end up in jail." "That's nice, dear."

Step 3. Emphasize the need for strong adverbs by writing the following on the board and asking students to match the situations with the correct descriptions.

1. Old man planting flowers in the hot sun   • He dug determinedly.
2. Prospector searching for gold   • He dug leisurely.
3. Murderer trying to hide latest victim's body   • He dug frantically.
4. City worker digging a trench for a pipe   • He dug methodically.

Step 4. Ask one student to come to the front of the room to act as Joe. Then assemble six others to function as a crowd. They are to allow Joe to pass as they would in any crowded venue. Ask Joe to do the following:

- to walk through the crowd
- to maneuver through the crowd
- to dance through the crowd
- to bulldoze his way through the crowd
- to slip through the crowd

Note the differences and discuss how using a strong verb adds to effective writing.

Step 5. Have students revise a piece of their own writing to make vocabulary strong and specific. Students might use Post-it notes or highlighters to indicate colorful word choice.

Developing Characters

In their fictional writing, your class is better at telling what characters are like rather than showing what they are like.

Goal

To challenge students to show rather than tell about character traits.

How to Reach It

Before you present the assignment sheet on the next page, review how professional authors reveal characters, the characters' words and actions being the most important ways. Students might find the assignment easier if they completed an analysis of the character first with a chart similar to this:

CHARACTER

_____

Character trait 1   Revealed when

_____

_____

Character trait 2   Revealed when

_____

_____

Character trait 3   Revealed when

_____

_____

Developing Characters

For each of the following scenarios, use separate paper to write a paragraph indicating your character's response.

1. Your character is stopped for speeding. Describe the scene with the police officer and the ensuing dialogue.

2. Your character has just won two million dollars in a lottery. What will he/she do with the money?

3. Your character answers the door to discover a pushy salesman. Describe the scene and the ensuing dialogue.

4. Your character is describing how he/she spent vacation time to a friend.

5. Your character is planning his/her ideal vacation. Write a description of it, being sure to include location, significant others, touring plans, and recreational pursuits.

6. Your character is eating out. Describe the restaurant chosen and the meal ordered.

7. Your character has decorated a favorite room. Describe this room and its uses.

8. Your character has died. Write the speech said at the funeral as well as an epitaph, a few words written in memory of a person usually on a tombstone.

9. Your character has one pet peeve. What is it and why does the character dislike that action or object so much?

Poetry Reading for Improved Poetry Writing

While your students are able to describe technique and meaning in poems that they read, their writing of poetry is limited.

Goal

To motivate students to improve their poetry writing through close reading of published poems.

How to Reach It

At the beginning of your study of poetry, encourage students to write poems. Let the students know that they will revise their poems several times throughout the term and that they will complete journal entries to explain the changes.

As students read poetry and learn about the link between meaning and literary technique, have them consider revision of their poems. For example, consider revision for effective word connotations as a follow-up to study of poems that contain evocative word connotations. Consider revision for original figures of speech as a follow-up to study of a poem in which original figures of speech are central to the poem's voice and meaning. Place particular emphasis on how poems conclude—often with a surprising twist. Challenge students to consider the most effective way to conclude their own poems.

In journal entries, students should explain their revisions. The final journal entry should comment on differences between the original and final version of the poem and why the final version represents an improvement.

Useful Reference

See *Teaching Poetry Writing to Adolescents* by Joseph Tsujimoto.

Spelling Demons

Your students do well enough when you give them spelling tests, yet they fail to demonstrate similar skill when it really matters — when they write.

Goal

To improve spelling in students' writing.

How to Reach It

Challenge individual students to learn about the strategies that work best for them. These strategies might include developing word pictures, using mnemonics, looking for the base word, and leaving blanks when they are uncertain about letters. Such strategies as well as spelling rules are elaborated clearly in Ruth Scott's *The Student Editor's Guide to Words*.

To encourage student engagement in the spelling challenge, have students keep a list of "spelling demons"—troublesome words—evident in their own writing. Ask students to identify strategies that they will use to deal with each demon. For example, some students benefit by writing the word with its misspelled part circled. Then students write the word correctly, close their eyes and take a mental picture of the word. Then students write out the word five times and rewrite the sentence in which the misspelling occurred, this time with the word correctly spelled.

If your class has regular spelling tests, have pairs of students test each other on their spelling demons. Some teachers combine full-class testing with such paired testing; for example, the teacher asks the large group to spell five words, then has student pairs test each other for five other words from their individual lists of demons.

Remind students to regularly edit their own writing with their spelling demons in mind. You might also post words that are high frequency or important in current study on classroom charts or create word walls to remind students of these words.

Useful Reference

Ruth Scott's *The Student Editor's Guide to Words* is an excellent resource for both you and your students.

Lessons in Usage from Students' Writing

You notice that students fail to catch important errors in usage when they edit their writing.

Goal

To motivate students to use their own writing and that of classmates to improve usage in their writing.

How to Reach It

As you mark student writing, use a coding system to indicate frequent usage errors you wish to work on with your class. For example, **1** might represent sentence fragments; **2**, errors with the apostrophe; **3**, unclear pronoun references.

Before you return papers to the class, have a volunteer handwrite appropriate coded sentences on overhead projector transparencies. In the above example, the volunteer could create an overhead transparency for sentence fragments, one for apostrophe errors, and one for unclear pronoun references. Each transparency would reflect the work of several students.

In instructing about these matters, remind students that the errors in usage occurred in their own writing. After working with the overhead transparencies, have students check their writing to make improvements related to instruction.

Useful Reference

Further suggestions about instruction in a variety of writing elements, including usage, can be found in *Student Self-Assessment* by Graham Foster.

Organization in Writing—Openers, Closers, Titles, and Transitions

When you ask your students to suggest ideas for effective titles, introductions, and conclusions, your response is a mouthing of silence.

Goal

To help students learn about techniques for effective organization in writing.

How to Reach It

The following page, "Organization in Writing," is best employed with effective examples—fiction and non-fiction studied by students as well as exemplars of student writing. Students should learn that the introductions and conclusions of narrative and expository text usually reflect quite different techniques. Following a consideration of examples, challenge students to identify techniques that they might use with a composition-in-progress.

Consistent with an earlier recommendation, you might have students employ Post-it notes or highlighters to signal techniques employed for titles, introductions, conclusions, and transitions.

Organization in Writing

OPTIONS FOR TITLES
- State topic literally.
- Symbolize a character or concept.
- Foreshadow something in the text.
- Achieve humor or irony.
- Capture attention with alliteration, a question or a play on words.

OPTIONS FOR INTRODUCTIONS

NARRATIVES
- Present a brief dialogue related to conflict.
- Plunge the reader into a conflict or dramatic event.
- Describe a setting to focus on movement or action related to the story's conflict.

ESSAYS
- Ask critical questions related to purpose and audience.
- Recount a brief, interesting story related to purpose and audience.
- State a startling fact or example related to purpose and audience.
- Tell about a foolish or incorrect view related to purpose and audience.
- Use an appropriate quotation.

TRANSITIONS AMONG PARAGRAPHS
- Use transition words such as "first," "in addition," and "finally."
- Briefly mention or refer to previous ideas.
- Repeat key words and phrases.

OPTIONS FOR CONCLUSIONS

NARRATIVES
- Recount final emotional response, reaction, or something learned from experience.
- Illustrate changes in attitudes or beliefs.
- Illustrate how the events might affect the protagonist's future.
- Conclude with a surprising twist.

ESSAYS
- Answer question posed in introduction.
- Warn the reader.
- Pose questions that still require answering.
- Make a surprising or powerful final point.
- Use an appropriate concluding quotation.
- Offer a prediction.

Moving into Expository Writing: Everybody's an Expert

Your students are more competent in their story writing than in expository writing.

Goal

To inspire confidence and competence as students engage in expository writing.

How to Reach It

A familiar nostrum for writing teachers is to invite students to tap into personal experience in their compositions. Tapping into personal experience is one powerful ingredient in developing expository writing skills, too. Having students write about their own expertise can be a comfortable way to teach them about expository writing.

In exploratory talk before the writing, suggest to students that all of them are experts in something and in different areas. Some students know about stamp collecting; others about hockey; others about sport card collecting; others about cooking.

The exploration of RAFTS writing variables—Role, Audience, Format, Topic and Strong Verb—on page 66 should help students focus. The complementary thought-web, page 67, is meant to help students explore the topic and to learn that key points require supporting details for a successful explanatory or expository text.

Students will probably need a second map to focus on their specifically chosen topic, purpose, and major points. You may find the blank photocopiable version of the form included on page 68 useful. It appears as an appendix.

RAFTS: Narrowing My Focus

R ROLE   I am an **expert** in _____

A AUDIENCE   I am writing this piece for the following audience _____

_____

F FORMAT   I am writing an *explanation.* _____

T TOPIC   I will focus on _____

S STRONG VERB   My purpose is to _____

_____ and to _____

EXAMPLE

R   Expert in First Aid

A   Students

F   Explanation

T   First Aid

S   to encourage students to learn first aid and to explain three first aid techniques

Thinking About Myself as an Expert

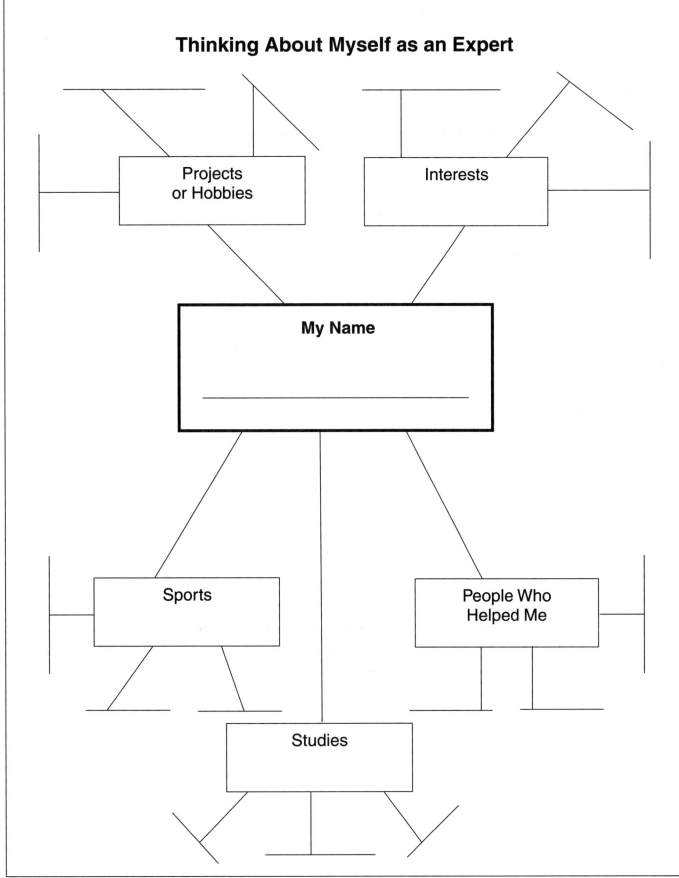

Purposeful Web Searches

Your class is employing computers to research a topic, in this case, ideas about first aid. You note that several students are random and inefficient in their Web searching. They are easily distracted and seem to be wasting time.

Goal

To encourage students to use their computer time wisely and effectively as they complete their research work.

How to Reach It

In exploring strategies for effective computer research, you might usefully emphasize the power of organizational strategies for the research. Before students begin their computer research, you might require them to respond to two questions:

1. What are my topic and purpose in completing the research?
2. What three or four questions do I consider most important in exploring the topic?

These questions should focus students in their research for information and help ensure that they make notes in response to the questions rather than randomly.

The following example illustrates the strategy. Note that if students are familiar with mapping, they could add more extensive detail to the sub points under the three question clusters. This strategy is also powerful in helping students write effective paragraphs. A blank version of the form appears as an appendix.

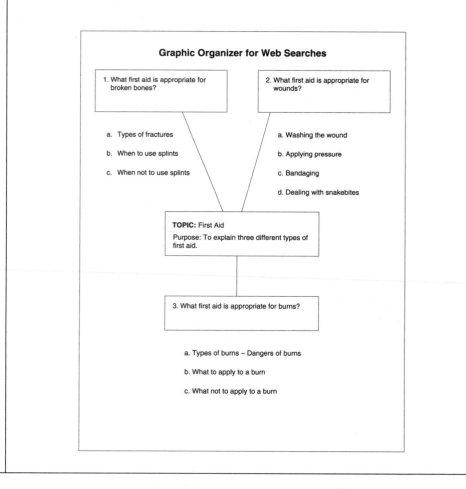

Graphic Organizer for Web Searches

1. What first aid is appropriate for broken bones?

   a. Types of fractures

   b. When to use splints

   c. When not to use splints

2. What first aid is appropriate for wounds?

   a. Washing the wound

   b. Applying pressure

   c. Bandaging

   d. Dealing with snakebites

TOPIC: First Aid
Purpose: To explain three different types of first aid.

3. What first aid is appropriate for burns?

   a. Types of burns – Dangers of burns

   b. What to apply to a burn

   c. What not to apply to a burn

Introductions with Pizzazz

When your students write expository text, their introductions are bland and colorless: "In this paper, my purpose is to. . . ."

Goal

To help students to write effective, engaging introductions.

How to Reach It

High school students typically learn about thesis statements or controlling ideas; younger students can usefully learn that the first paragraph of a piece of expository writing should offer a preview of what follows. It's easier for students to present an interesting preview when they begin the first paragraph of a piece of expository writing with a snappy sentence. Especially for inexperienced expository writers, be sure to review the techniques listed on the next page. Have students attach a Post-it note comment to the first paragraph of any expository composition. On the Post-it note, they should indicate the technique employed to capture attention.

How to Write Opening Sentences for Expository Text

TECHNIQUE

EXAMPLE

A. Ask a question.

Do you feel inadequate when you speak in public?

B. State a startling fact.

Few people would know how to survive if they became lost in the wilderness.

C. State a foolish or incorrect view.

Many people believe that the Internet is just for technical experts or "geeks." Nothing could be more ridiculous; everybody can benefit from using the Internet.

D. Use an effective quotation.

"We are our brother's keeper." Because human beings are at their best when they care for one another, all of us should learn first aid so that we can help in emergencies.

Do We Have To?

You present the class with a strategy for completing a task, in this case, a pre-writing strategy for story writing. The strategy invites students to consider the following key elements of the story:

Somebody _____
Wanted _____
But _____
So _____

Several students whine that they already know how to write stories and don't want to use the strategy. You decide to avoid the "Do it my way . . . or else" response, but want to make it clear to students that pre-writing is valuable and that all students should reflect before drafting.

Goal

To help students understand that while they have a choice of strategies to complete tasks, they should choose responsibly.

How to Reach It

You are always wise to separate skill requirements from student choices of strategies. In the example of a narrative assignment at left, writers are required to create a story with a protagonist who must deal with a clearly defined problem that is resolved. Teachers know that many student writers fail to clearly establish a conflict in their stories and, if they do, fail to resolve it. All of this is a matter of skill—the outcomes expected in the assignment.

Strategies, which refer to how one proceeds to complete a task, should *always* be optional. Teachers know that strategies vary from learner to learner. In the above example, the teacher has offered one pre-writing strategy. The teacher might wisely ask the class, "Can you think of other ways to plan your story?" Students should certainly be free to employ other viable options. In this classroom example, some students may prefer a graphic representation of the story's conflict, rising action, climax, and resolution. These visual learners should be encouraged to make such representations.

If students pose the "Do we have to?" question, answer that the task, a curriculum requirement, is probably non-negotiable, but how they proceed with it is an individual option. Still, remind students to choose wisely since a poor choice has unfortunate consequences. They might analyze their task by considering these headings:

SKILLS	HOW
What I have to do to succeed in the assignment	How I will proceed to succeed in the assignment (sequence)

Regular goal-setting activities help students reflect on the efficacy of their choices.

Useful Reference

For further discussion of skills, strategies, and choice of options to complete a task, refer to *I Think, Therefore I Learn!*, a book on metacognition.

How Do the Pros Do It?

In your students' minds, reading and writing are disconnected; however, you know that if they attended to techniques used by authors in texts being read, their writing would likely improve.

Goal

To focus students on using published writing to learn specific techniques for their own writing.

How to Reach It

Challenge students to use texts being read to learn about specific techniques to improve their writing. The sheets "Using Texts to Answer Questions About Writing" and "How Do the Pros Do It?" invite students to formulate key questions to answer with the help of familiar texts, possibly from anthologies of literature. It is best to have them deal with just one question until they get used to the strategy. Have them adopt the following sequence:

Step 1. Write down your question about your writing. For example: "How can I make the beginning of my story interesting for the reader?"

Step 2. Find examples of how other authors deal with the question. (See "How Do the Pros Do It?" as answered by a Grade 5 student on page 74. A photocopiable version appears as an appendix.)

Step 3. Explain what the authors do.

Step 4. Explain how the authors have helped you to answer your question.

Using Texts to Answer Questions About Writing

Using texts that you are reading to help you improve your writing or to answer any of your questions about writing is a useful strategy. The idea is to consider how some of the authors whose books you have read address the concerns that you have as a writer.

Think about some books that you are familiar with or have been reading lately. How do the authors deal with some of the writing issues noted below? Focus on an issue that especially interests you. Explain how the authors' writing choices help you answer your question.

- creating interest at the beginning of a story

- presenting details of setting

- creating interesting/believable dialogue

- structuring a story

- developing conflict

- ending a story

- using quotation marks in dialogue

- using different kinds of sentences

- using descriptive language effectively

- letting the author's own personality show in the writing

- showing rather than telling

How Do the Pros Do It?

I have this question about my own writing:

How can I make the beginning of my story interesting?

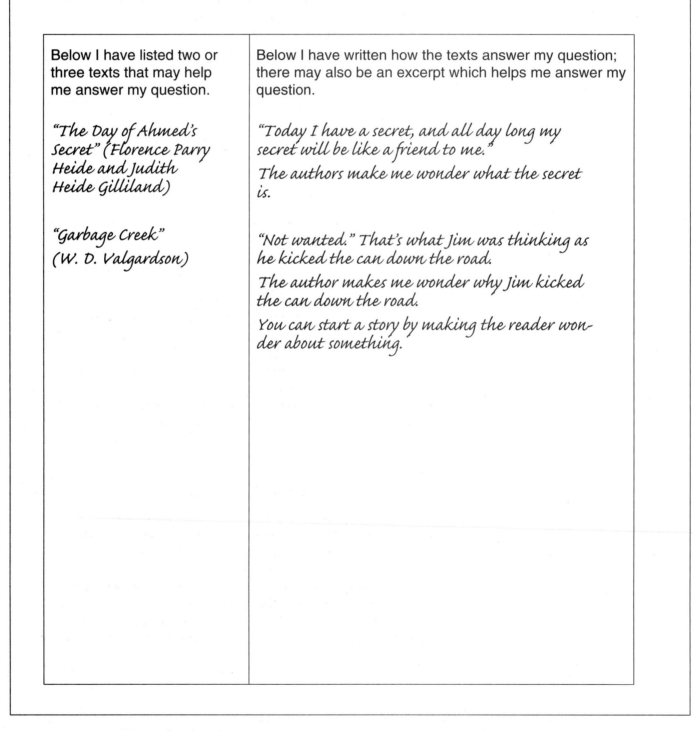

Below I have listed two or three texts that may help me answer my question.	Below I have written how the texts answer my question; there may also be an excerpt which helps me answer my question.
"The Day of Ahmed's Secret" (Florence Parry Heide and Judith Heide Gilliland)	*"Today I have a secret, and all day long my secret will be like a friend to me."* *The authors make me wonder what the secret is.*
"Garbage Creek" (W. D. Valgardson)	*"Not wanted." That's what Jim was thinking as he kicked the can down the road.* *The author makes me wonder why Jim kicked the can down the road.* *You can start a story by making the reader wonder about something.*

Helping Students Understand Themselves as Writers

Your students are stagnant in their writing skills and are unable to identify strategies to improve their writing.

Goal

To promote improved writing skills by having students identify personally effective writing strategies.

How to Reach It

The large goal of improving writing skills embeds a range of instructional strategies. Just as you are wise to emphasize metacognition to develop reading skills, you are wise to emphasize it to develop writing skills. Metacognitive writers are able to describe how they complete writing tasks and how they proceed before, during, and after the drafting of a specific composition. Obviously, students should identify different strategies for different writing tasks.

Language arts professional literature frequently describes a viable writing process according to what effective writers do before, during, and after writing. It's a good idea if you adopt this terminology to describe writing strategies and challenge your students to use similar terminology to describe the strategies that work for them.

BEFORE DRAFTING

These strategies recognize that writers need to discover and to focus on what they have to say in a composition.

- Activating/building background knowledge about topic and form for the composition
- Engaging in exploratory writing: sometimes called free-writing or journal writing, this kind of writing focuses on discovery rather than communication. (Sometimes, ideas or experiences revealed through exploratory writing can be taken to final draft.)
- Determining writing variables: variables include purpose, audience, format, topic, and role for the writing.
- Choosing a pre-writing approach: alternatives include using graphic organizers, brainstorming, completing research notes, and free-writing.

DURING DRAFTING

These strategies remind writers to "keep the flow going."

- Writing on every other line: doing this encourages revision.
- Beginning at the most comfortable part of the composition: writers are reminded that writing sequence is a personal choice and that writers often write the introduction last.
- Leaving blank spaces where words don't come: it's more important to get ideas on paper than to refine expression.
- Rereading what one has written before continuing the draft
- Referring to pre-writing notes and modifying them

AFTER DRAFTING

These strategies remind students that effective writers learn to be their own critical readers.

- Rereading for clarity: writers should focus on the clarity of their expression and organization, on their vocabulary and sentence pattern choices, and on matters of spelling, punctuation, and grammar usage.
- Conferring with others to improve the writing: some writers prefer to revise with partner help; others do not.
- Applying specific criteria appropriate to purpose, audience, format, topic, and role for the writing.

As with assessment of reading strategies, some teachers make assessment of writing strategies part of their assessment of writing products. In conferences or written reports, your students could note the strategies employed before, during, and after the drafting of a specific text. That would let you determine the extent to which they can describe and monitor their personal writing process. You can emphasize the key point: that students who are able to describe their writing strategies write more effectively.

The reflection tool on the following page may be employed to encourage metacognitive writing.

Useful Reference

For further information about writing strategies and metacognition, see *I Think, Therefore I Learn!*

Understanding Myself as a Writer

Title of Text   *Newspaper Article*

Strategies I used before drafting:

I first used a graphic organizer. I also used RAFTS and focused on the topic.

Strategies I used during drafting:

Focusing on the topic.
No using dull words and listing words.
Form a picture in the reader's mind.

Strategies that I employed after drafting:

Going over the spelling, tense, and sentence structure.
Replacing ordinary words with more descriptive words.
Read it over.
Punctuate.

My goals for future writing:

Writing stories that people will want to read over and over.

What I have learned about myself as a writer:

I can express my feelings and thoughts while writing.

Learning Contracts for Differentiated Instruction

Your class contains students of wide-ranging abilities. While some students struggle with reading and writing, some students read and write well beyond grade level expectations.

Goal

To employ learning contracts as a technique for differentiated instruction.

How to Reach It

One way to differentiate instruction is to allow class time for students to fulfill learning contracts, such as that by a Grade 4 student below. These contracts specify topic, goals, resources, assessment, and time allowed. For instance, a student or group of students might contract to create a comic strip. Another student might write advice columns. Someone else might use a handbook to help with targeted writing features, such as paragraphing. Time allowed reflects the complexity of the task. A photocopiable form appears as an appendix.

Learning contracts work most effectively when students enjoy access to extensive collections of handbooks and anthologies. Teachers may also employ file folders with needs-related exercises that students can complete as part of their learning contracts. Furthermore, many learning contracts can be completed with Internet resources.

Report on Kateri Tekakwitha

Learning Contract

Name ___*Maria*___ Class ___*Gr. 4*___

TOPIC/GOALS

I agree to use the time allowed to work on the following challenge:
For my report I will have three sources of information, make an outline and "jot" notes and see if I can make a report from there.

TIME ALLOWED

I agree to have the work completed by *May 21 (two weeks)*

RESOURCES

I will use the following print, Internet, media, and human resources to complete the project:
I will use three sources of information: at least two books and one Internet article. I will use Lily of the Mohawks and an Internet article written by Margaret Bunson.

ASSESSMENT

My work will be assessed as follows:

Title page: /3	*Introduction:* /5	*Three themes:* /15
Conclusion: /5	*Bibliography:* /2	*Punctuation:* /5

Note: If a rubric has been agreed to, I will submit a self-assessment of my work with the rubric.

Writing Variables and Voice in Writing

Student writing, including report writing, in various subjects is wooden and voiceless.

Goal

To motivate students to think about writing variables to add color and voice to their writing.

How to Reach It

Encourage students to write about topics in a wider variety of roles, in a wider variety of audiences, in a wider variety of purposes, and in a wider variety of formats. Rather than having them write a typical report about the circulatory system, let them write a letter in the role of a mature red blood cell to the audience of a younger red blood cell about interesting points of call as it travels throughout the body. Rather than having them write about schooling in Japan, let them create a diary entry by a 12-year-old Japanese student to describe a typical day.

The earlier mentioned RAFTS strategy can be used to help students focus their writing on voice.

R	ROLE	From whose point of view am I writing? My own? Someone else's?
A	AUDIENCE	To whom am I writing? What is my relationship to this audience? Do I need to be formal or casual in my writing?
F	FORMAT	What particular writing form is appropriate or assigned? In other words, am I writing a story, an expository essay, a business letter, or something else?
T	TOPIC	What am I writing about?
S	STRONG VERB	What is my purpose? What exactly am I seeking to achieve in my writing?

Students gain two major advantages by reviewing RAFTS variables: they focus on the writing task and they discover ideas for their composition. The following pair of essays, "Christmas Pickpocket—The Victim" and "Christmas Pickpocket—The Villain," were written by the same author. They can be employed to illustrate how a single topic is affected when presented from a different role. Have students consider how the content for any given topic will change with a change in role or audience.

Christmas Pickpocket—The Victim

December 24 was our last chance to finish our Christmas shopping before we returned home to Istanbul. Darlene and I had spent four enjoyable days visiting the City of Lights and set out on our final excursion before heading to the airport.

We were staying near the Eiffel Tower in a nice safe neighborhood and had become experts on using the Paris Metro system. The LaMotte–Grenelle line was near our hotel and was the fastest route to the Lafayette Shopping Centre. We pushed through the turnstiles and proceeded down the stairs to the platform. There was no train waiting, so we sat on the bench near the bottom of the stairs. I was feeling a little tired as I was still fighting the effects of an ear infection and a head cold.

The platform was quiet with only a few waiting passengers. In a minute the train could be heard rumbling down the tracks toward our station. It raced into the station and the last car stopped a few feet up the track past the spot where we had been sitting. We hustled over to the door and stepped into the last car.

In the next ten seconds it seemed as if a thousand things happened. Just as I stepped into the train, I heard a sharp clink as if something metal had fallen on the floor of the train. I looked down quickly and could see nothing. At the same time, I felt pushed gently from behind as if the person who had dropped the metal object, which I never saw, seemed to be scrambling to pick it up. I thought instantly that it was strange that this guy was in such a hurry to push and scurry around my feet to pick whatever it was up when the train was not crowded and I would have been glad to move over to the side. But he kept rummaging around near my feet and I thought that it was very strange behavior. Suddenly, a reflex from nowhere made me tap on my back right-hand pocket to check if my wallet was there. It wasn't. I quickly whirled around and looked directly at a young dark-haired man standing inches away from me. Again, for no conscious reason, my right hand reached out and grabbed the arm of the young man. There were no conscious thoughts about robbery or pickpockets or thieves. It must have been the subconscious mind that has read Oliver Twist and remembered the pickpocket lessons of Fagan or the countless episodes of Hill Street Blues or NYPD Blues that told me what had happened.

As I grabbed the young man's arm, he smiled and said "Sorry" and he lifted his other hand up in the air and it contained a light brown wallet. It was mine! There was an incredulous millisecond where I was stunned to see my wallet held lightly in this stranger's hand. I let go his arm and snatched my wallet from him. I took my other hand and opened it to see that everything was there, my money, my credit cards, and my Turkish residency permit. When I looked back up, the young man had stepped back off the train and the doors were closing. He again smiled at me and walked away as the train lurched away to the next station.

My heart rate was normal, I was not sweating, and I felt totally in control. I never saw the other guy. And the rest of the people on the train who saw what happened looked vacant, detached and possibly oblivious. It was a ten second adventure that elevated me from old geezer to cool crime fighter! Wow!

Christmas Pickpocket—The Villain

December 24 is a great day for business. My buddy Jean-Claude and I are professional pickpockets who work the Paris Underground. On the day of Christmas Eve, the streets are packed with last-minute Christmas shoppers with plenty of cash looking for last-minute bargains.

We work the station at La Motte–Grenelle for a number of reasons. The steps from the street lead directly down onto the platform and consequently provide a quick means of escape if something should go wrong. You don't want to pick a station where you are a long distance from street level and the chance of some hero interfering, if you have to make a quick getaway. And since LaMotte is near the Eiffel Tower the large number of tourists make for a lot of easy targets.

As we descended the steps into the Metro, our gaze fell upon an old man with short white hair slumped on a bench near the bottom of the steps. He was dressed in a fairly expensive leather coat with a map book of Paris in his pocket screaming out "tourist." He appeared to be very slow moving and would not be much of a problem. As we heard the sound of the approaching train, we began to maneuver into position.

The old man, accompanied by his wife, rose slowly but shuffled quickly toward the opening door of the last compartment. Jean-Claude moved in close behind the man and I waited a few steps further back. The art of the pickpocket is swift, precise and carefully practised. Jean-Claude "accidentally" dropped his rich-looking gold cigarette lighter between the feet of the old man just as he stepped into the train. The lighter clinked and the old man stopped and looked down to see what it was. JC blocked the old man's advance and pretended to be picking up the lighter between the man's feet. The victim was startled at the mild bumping of the man on the floor and did not feel me slide in close behind him. As JC continued to make a show of pushing on and around the victim's feet, groping for his lighter, I gently bumped the man, lifted his jacket and extracted his thick brown wallet in an instant. Another heist pulled to perfection.

Then the tables turned! In the wink of an eye, the old man whirled around quickly and looked coldly into my eyes. His right arm, like a bionic weapon, shot out and grasped my right arm with incredible pressure. This was no ordinary tourist. He must have been a policeman, private eye, or veteran agent to have interpreted what was occurring so quickly. His grasp tightened and his cool eyes did not blink. I knew I was in trouble. I had only one choice as his grip on my arm tightened. With my left hand I held up his wallet for him to see and murmured "sorry." He remained silent and focused. In one motion, the old man released his vise-like grip on my arm and snatched his wallet from my surrendering hand. The wail of the train warning that the doors were about to close sounded. During the next second, the old man's steely eyes dropped for an instant to examine the contents of his wallet and I took advantage and stepped back off the train. The swish of the closing doors and the thud as they locked made my heart skip. The old man did not move but just continued to gaze coldly at me through the train window.

Jean-Claude and I raced up the stairs to the street and safety. This victim was no ordinary tourist but I will never know who he was!

Adding Color and Voice to Writing

Student writing in your class is competent, but dull and voiceless. You and the students have agreed to emphasize voice in subsequent writing assignments.

Goal

To encourage students to develop voice as writers.

How to Reach It

Review the essential characteristics of voice in writing:

- emotional response;
- honesty;
- realistic portrayal of speech patterns in fiction;
- unique choice of detail, vocabulary, and imagery.

One way to focus on voice is to choose an exemplar or piece of student writing that is strong in voice. Create a modified cloze exercise by whiting out a few words and phrases that demonstrate uniqueness, that is, voice. Then have students consider the author's original. An example, entitled "Used," follows.

In addition, have students apply voice-specific criteria to a piece of writing.

A list of self-assessment criteria appears on page 85 and a rubric for voice is on page 86.

Used

It was nineteen eighty-eight, more importantly the beginning of grade eight. I walked to school with all of my school supplies hunched over my back in a bag. I crunched all of the leaves under my canoe-sized feet. I don't know about everyone else but I loved the sound. It's too bad I hated school. I couldn't help but think of the year ahead of me. I only wished it would be as easy as grade seven. Too bad I was so bored with my school. I followed my teacher's directions to my new class.

Immediately I began scoping out my class, and the girls! I noticed a new girl who looked very get-to-knowable. I then was diverted, almost mechanically, to the row on the other side of me. There I noticed this girl who had the most gorgeous face in the world. Well, maybe not that gorgeous, but her eyes were so tranquil that I fell in love with her almost immediately.

I went over and reunited with my platoon of pals. We swapped our stories of couch lounging, almost competing! Then I started to think about this girl again. I asked my friends what they thought about her . . . they didn't even notice.

The next couple of days all I could do was _____. I would stare at this girl constantly. I would get an occasional urge to listen, but it was curbed by her subtleness and beauty.

I was in Home Ec. Class and so was she. I was PRIMO LUCKY! I STARED AT HER ACROSS THE TABLE, AND SHE STARTED TO STARE BACK. She smiled, AND I was captivated. I was her _____.

After school that day, I started to get to know her. She offered to walk with me to the bus stop, so I said yes, and we were on our way. Once there she revealed that she had no money for the bus and she needed to go downtown. So I handed her my bus pass. This meant that I had to walk, but I waited with her anyway. When the bus finally came, I put on my thinking _____. I told the bus driver that I had forgotten my bus pass at home, but he did not let me on. So I had to walk miles home for her. Did she just use me?

The next morning I had to walk to school. Upon my arrival, I approached her and asked for my bus pass. It was a relief just to see it.

Later that month she did it again. _____.

Grade 9 Student

Used

It was nineteen eighty-eight, more importantly the beginning of grade eight. I walked to school with all of my school supplies hunched over my back in a bag. I crunched all of the leaves under my canoe-sized feet. I don't know about everyone else but I loved the sound. It's too bad I hated school. I couldn't help but think of the year ahead of me. I only wished it would be as easy as grade seven. Too bad I was so bored with my school. I followed my teacher's directions to my new class.

Immediately I began scoping out my class, and the girls! I noticed a new girl who looked very get-to-knowable. I then was diverted, almost mechanically, to the row on the other side of me. There I noticed this girl who had the most gorgeous face in the world. Well, maybe not that gorgeous, but her eyes were so tranquil that I fell in love with her almost immediately.

I went over and reunited with my platoon of pals. We swapped our stories of couch lounging, almost competing! Then I started to think about this girl again. I asked my friends what they thought about her . . . they didn't even notice.

The next couple of days all I could do was drool. I would stare at this girl constantly. I would get an occasional urge to listen, but it was curbed by her subtleness and beauty.

I was in Home Ec. Class and so was she. I was PRIMO LUCKY! I STARED AT HER ACROSS THE TABLE, AND SHE STARTED TO STARE BACK. She smiled, AND I was captivated. I was her mindless vegetable.

After school that day, I started to get to know her. She offered to walk with me to the bus stop, so I said yes, and we were on our way. Once there she revealed that she had no money for the bus and she needed to go downtown. So I handed her my bus pass. This meant that I had to walk, but I waited with her anyway. When the bus finally came, I put on my thinking sombrero. I told the bus driver that I had forgotten my bus pass at home, but he did not let me on. So I had to walk miles home for her. Did she just use me?

The next morning I had to walk to school. Upon my arrival, I approached her and asked for my bus pass. It was a relief just to see it.

Later that month she did it again. I caught on after the third time.

Grade 9 Student

Self-Assessment of Writing for Voice

Use Post-it notes on your writing to indicate the following:

- the sentence that most shows that you care about the topic;

- details that others probably wouldn't think of using;

- the sentence that best conveys your feelings or your character's feelings;

- two words that are unique, interesting, and maybe even funny (if appropriate);

- the sentence that best captures your tone of voice or the tone of voice of your characters;

- the sentence in which you most effectively show rather than tell.

A Rubric for Voice in Writing

	Level 4 Proficient	Level 3 Competent	Level 2 Novice	Level 1 Weak
HONESTY AND CARING	Consistently demonstrates caring about the topic and an honest, personal consideration of it.	Regularly demonstrates caring about the topic and an honest, personal consideration of it.	Sometimes demonstrates caring about the topic and an honest, personal consideration of it.	Rarely demonstrates caring about the topic and an honest, personal consideration of it.
EMOTION	Consistently implies emotions appropriate to the text.	Regularly implies emotions appropriate to the text.	Sometimes implies emotions appropriate to the text.	Rarely implies emotions appropriate to the text.
DICTION	Consistently employs unique and appropriate words and consistently avoids clichés.	Regularly employs unique and appropriate words and usually avoids clichés.	Sometimes employs unique and appropriate words and sometimes uses clichés.	Rarely employs unique and appropriate words and frequently uses clichés.
DETAIL AND IMAGERY	Consistently chooses appropriate, unique detail and images.	Regularly chooses appropriate, unique detail and images.	Sometimes chooses appropriate, unique detail and images.	Rarely chooses unique detail and images.
SOUND	Read aloud, the writing consistently captures the tone of characters' voices or the author's voice.	Read aloud, the writing regularly captures the tone of characters' voices or the author's voice.	Read aloud, the writing sometimes captures the tone of characters' voices or the author's voice.	Read aloud, the writing rarely captures the tone of characters' voices or the author's voice.

Part C   Speaking and Listening

While speaking and listening skills are sometimes overlooked in schooling, teachers increasingly recognize that speaking and listening are important life skills and are often the foundation for success in reading and writing tasks. The idea bank entries here deal with speaking and listening in both formal and informal contexts.

Encouraging Student Listening

These activities help students recognize the importance of listening, especially to instructions on how to complete tasks.

- **Are You Listening?** (pages 88–89)
- **Explaining in Their Own Words** (page 90)

Benefiting from Oral Interpretation

Formal oral presentations are a current program requirement. The activities in this section suggest that thoughtful oral presentations benefit reading and writing as well.

- **Not Round-Robin Reading Again!** (pages 91–92)
- **An Alternative to High-Interest, Low Vocabulary Texts** (page 93)
- **Creating and Performing Scripts** (pages 94–95)
- **A Variation of Readers' Theatre** (page 96)

Exploring Group Dynamics

Group work and cooperative learning are receiving increased emphasis as program requirements, possibly because educators and business leaders recognize teamwork as an important life skill. The idea bank entries in this section focus on helping students work effectively with others.

- **Parameters for Effective Group Behavior** (pages 97–98)
- **Talking About Text** (page 99)
- **Discussing Thinking Strategies** (page 100)
- **Think-Pair-Share and Jigsaw Approaches** (page 101)

Are You Listening?

You lead a class discussion to review content recently studied. As you question the class and invite students to pose their own questions, you make notes on the blackboard. As soon as someone poses a question, one or two students raise their hands quickly. Others are indifferent or inattentive. A few students are chatting quietly about matters unrelated to the review lesson.

Goal

To motivate your students to participate thoughtfully in classroom discussions.

How to Reach It

To focus all students on the review questions, begin the review by asking the class to write answers to questions as they are raised in discussion. Warn students that, since time is limited, they should work efficiently. Monitor students to ensure participation in the activity. Remember that the most fundamental principle for encouraging students to listen is to require action related to listening. You might ask students to report on a key point added to their notes during the class discussion.

During sharing of key points added to notes, choose students who may not be the first to volunteer. Ask all students to explain new understandings of the content.

Following the review, challenge students to consider ways in which the answers to the questions can be organized. A graphic organizer, such as the one on the following page, may be useful.

Useful Reference

Thinking Visually: Step-by-Step Exercises That Promote Visual, Auditory and Kinesthetic Learning by Oliver Caviglioli and Ian Harris offers a systematic treatment of graphic organizers.

Organizational Map for Information

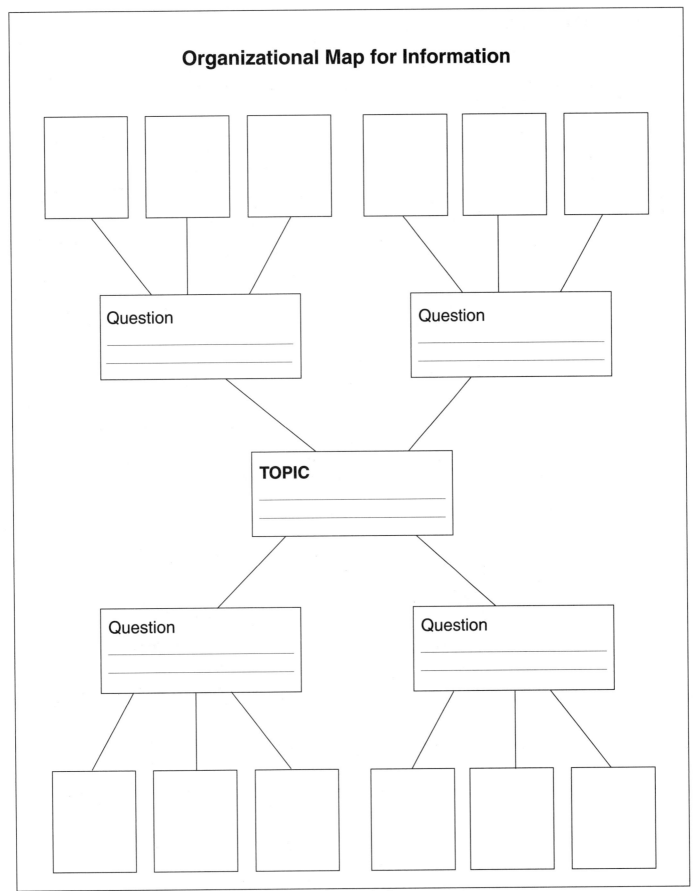

Question
_____
_____

Question
_____
_____

TOPIC
_____
_____

Question
_____
_____

Question
_____
_____

Explaining in Their Own Words

Immediately after presenting an assignment to the class, you notice that many students are wasting time. Some students doodle on blank paper, obviously unsure about how to proceed. Others begin to work, but do not seem to have a clear plan.

Goal

To encourage students to be task centred as they complete assignments.

How to Reach It

As part of introducing a new assignment, engage students in a paraphrasing or retelling activity. Pick students to explain the task in their own words. After the first interpretation, let other students add, delete, modify, or confirm the previous interpretation. "I agree with the previous explanation" is not an acceptable statement.

An imaginative variation of this idea involves students sitting in a circle. You toss a beanbag to a student who shares his or her understanding of the assignment. The student then tosses the beanbag to another student for another interpretation and so on.

After these paraphrasing/retelling activities, you might ask students to write the assignment in their notebooks and to fill in a sequence chart for completing it. Many students are visual learners so graphic organizers related to work-in-progress will help them focus and plan effectively. If need be, a sequence chart similar to the one below can be completed by the entire class; a photocopiable version appears as an appendix.

Useful References

Collections of graphic organizers can be found in *Thinking Visually* by Oliver Caviglioli and Ian Harris, *New Directions in Reading Instruction* by Bess Hinson, and *Responses to Literature, Grades K–8*, by James Macon, Diane Bewell, and Mary Ellen Vogt.

Assignment Completion Sequence

The Assignment *A book report*

Important Requirements _____

_____

Due Date *October 6*

Sequence

Date		
October 1	1.	*First I will re-look over my book and plan the report.*
October 1	2.	*Next I will do planning such as RAFTS, main ideas, and other things.*
October 2	3.	*Then I will write my rough draft.*
October 3	4.	*Then I will edit for vocabulary, content, sentence structure, grammar and I will make sure my writing fits the criteria for the assignment.*
October 5	5.	*Once I am happy with my rough draft and have it edited, I will finalize my draft by rewriting it as my good draft, then hand it in.*

Not Round-Robin Reading Again!

Round-robin reading, in which students take turns reading an unfamiliar text, is a trial for many students. While some students read new texts fluently, many stumble on words and read at a painfully slow pace.

Goal

To achieve a more positive oral reading experience for all of your students, an oral reading experience that clearly enhances reading comprehension.

How to Reach It

Instead of round-robin reading, call upon students to prepare oral interpretations of literature. Students may prepare their readings as much as they want. While you may decide to assign texts for prepared reading, students should sometimes select their own texts. For instance, in the study of poetry, why not challenge all students to choose a poem they like, read it to the class, and comment on why they like it?

It is a good idea to review elements of effective oral interpretation of text, as outlined below.

- *Respect punctuation clues.* Do not pause unnaturally. A comma signals a pause; a period indicates a stop. Exclamation marks signal an excited or surprised tone; question marks signal an inquisitive tone, and, in some cases, a tone of outrage, disbelief, or command. How do punctuation marks guide the reading of the selected texts?

   Many teachers would argue that oral interpretation activities are the most effective way to teach punctuation since punctuation is nothing more than a set of signals showing the reader how to handle the flow of words as a speaker would say them. When we write, we punctuate with pen, pencil, or word-processor; when we speak, we punctuate with our voice.
- *Decide about timing and pacing.* Timing and pacing relate to the rate at which we read lines. A change of pace affects emotional response and commands attention. How quickly or slowly should the text be read? Will there be a change in timing or pacing for the selected text?
- *Decide about volume.* Different texts require different volume and sometimes changes in volume. How loudly or softly should lines be read?
- *Decide about emphasis.* An effective oral interpretation always moves towards a focal point. Audiences must feel that the reading is building to a climax. What is the most important or intense point to be emphasized in the reading?

As part of your instruction, be sure to model effective use of these elements in your own oral interpretations.

Oral interpretation of literature fosters a close reading of text; close reading is required for reading comprehension. The rubric on the following page may be employed for self-assessment, for peer-assessment, and for the teacher's assessment of the oral interpretation.

Useful References

Good-bye Round Robin by Michael Opitz and Timothy Rasinski presents a range of oral reading strategies and identifies texts that work well for performed oral reading. *Literacy Techniques* by David Booth includes information on the oral interpretation of literature and a range of practical strategies on a variety of topics. *Stories to Read Aloud*, also by David Booth, is a rich source of texts meant to be read aloud.

A Rubric for Oral Interpretation of Literature

	Level 4 Proficient	Level 3 Competent	Level 2 Novice	Level 1 Weak
PREPARATION	Demonstrates thoughtful preparation of oral interpretation.	Demonstrates considerable preparation of oral interpretation.	Demonstrates limited preparation of oral interpretation.	Demonstrates little preparation of oral interpretation.
PUNCTUATION CUES	Interprets all punctuation cues.	Interprets most punctuation cues.	Interprets a few punctuation cues.	Disregards punctuation cues.
TIMING AND PACING	Consistently uses timing and pacing for appropriate emphasis.	Usually uses timing and pacing for appropriate emphasis.	Sometimes uses appropriate timing and pacing for appropriate emphasis.	Seldom uses timing and pacing for appropriate emphasis.
VOLUME	Consistently uses appropriate volume and appropriate variation of volume.	Usually uses appropriate volume and appropriate variation of volume.	Sometimes uses appropriate volume and appropriate variation of volume.	Seldom uses appropriate volume and appropriate variation of volume.
EMPHASIS	Clearly indicates focal point and builds to focal point.	Indicates focal point and builds to focal point.	Hints at focal point.	Fails to build to focal point.

An Alternative to High-Interest, Low Vocabulary Texts

Some of your students are reading far below grade-level expectations. They are frustrated when expected to independently read selections in their anthology as well as novels that you have chosen for the class.

Goal

To use books-on-tape as an alternative to high-interest, low vocabulary texts.

How to Reach It

For many years Language Arts teachers have employed high-interest, low vocabulary texts with students reading below grade level. While such resources, readily available from educational resource outlets, may be appropriate, do not overlook books-on-tape as an alternative. Taped books with accompanying print texts are increasingly available. Often, these taped books feature competent and expressive oral reading, sometimes by actors.

When students use books-on-tape, they can gain the advantage of using grade-level resources in a manageable medium. The rule is that they must follow the print text as they listen. This method helps them to associate the sound of words with the corresponding print symbols, which is critical if they are to improve their reading ability.

Encourage your school librarian to expand the school's collection of books-on-tape. For texts unavailable in audiotaped format, you might seek out a competent volunteer to prepare a tape of selections from your literature anthology or from any other source.

You might also consider recording effective examples of oral interpretation of literature, including readers' theatre, by your students. Not only would these recordings be useful exemplars to communicate expectations and possibilities, they would also serve as local contributions to your school's books-on-tape collection. The readers' scripts should be available with the recordings so that a student can follow the script while listening to the recording.

Creating and Performing Scripts

Your students love to perform. However, they are limited in their reading skills.

Goal

To have students use performance skills to improve close reading of a text.

How to Reach It

As your class discusses narrative text, ask them to choose a brief section that is particularly noteworthy for its presentation of conflict between or among characters. Have students work in groups with the same number of students as characters to transform the section into a dramatic script. They will likely want to stay close to the dialogue within the original text, but may make additions and deletions as appropriate. An example, based on the popular young adult novel *Ellen Foster*, follows.

Challenge students in their groups to perform their scenes to reveal the characters' feelings and to illustrate the conflict. They might learn their lines by heart or take a readers' theatre approach (see the next idea bank entry).

If you prefer a shorter activity, you could transform the narrative text into script or have someone else make the transformation. With this approach, several groups could act out the script to note different interpretations of characters' feelings and conflict.

A Scene from *Ellen Foster* by Kaye Gibbons

Ellen: So if you two would sit there on the couch and hide your eyes I have something I want to give you. Just let me go back into my room and I'll be right back.

....

Ellen: So what do you think?

Nadine: Why, Ellen that is really nice.

Dora: Did you trace the cats?

Ellen: No, Dora. I painted them all my own self for you and your Mama to hang in your living room or anywhere you see fit.

Dora: It looks like you traced them.

Ellen: No, Dora. I drew these kitties with you in mind.

Nadine: They look so sweet. I'll hang the picture first thing tomorrow.

Ellen: What's wrong with right now?

Nadine: It needs a frame, Honey. A picture as pretty as that needs a frame.

Ellen: But the store won't open tomorrow on account of Christmas. Anyway I took care of that already. (*fans out colored paper frames.*) You can have the frame of your choice. I'll assemble the whole business here tonight.

Dora: Mama, you don't plan to put some old tacky paper frame on the wall, do you?

Nadine: Be nice to Ellen, Dora. This is all so cute.

Ellen walks away.

A Variation of Readers' Theatre

Your students have done less work on improving their speaking skills than with improving their reading and writing skills. You want them to improve their formal speaking ability.

Goal

To employ readers' theatre to improve students' speaking skills.

How to Reach It

Many teachers see readers' theatre as a favorite vehicle for improving students' oral language skills. Their reason is that readers' theatre is a manageable instructional strategy. Furthermore, it focuses directly on voice production factors rather than on other theatrical elements, such as costumes, sets, and props.

Through modelling and discussion, help students understand the essential challenge of readers' theatre: to employ voice to suggest a character's thoughts, feelings, responses, and conflict. The elements of effective oral interpretation are outlined under "Not Round-Robin Reading Again!" on page 91.

Let groups of students decide on how to involve team members most effectively in the performance of the text. One reader may take several parts.

While readers' theatre performances can be elaborate with students reading from notebooks of uniform shape and color, employing music stands, and possibly sitting at different heights, many Language Arts teachers simplify readers' theatre activities through the following sequence:

Step 1. Select a readers' theatre text. It need not be a dramatic text. Usually, it is a novel or short story. Alternatively, you may decide to involve students in the selection.

Step 2. Have groups of students discuss the characters' feelings, beliefs, conflicts, and motivations.

Step 3. Let group members decide on assignment of parts for performance of the reading. If they are not working with a script, they need to decide on how the text will be divided. In either case, students should decide whether they need a reader for stage directions or non-dialogue parts of a fictional text.

Step 4. Ask group members to practise different ways of speaking the parts, experimenting with volume, speed, and intonation.

Step 5. In teacher and peer feedback to the readers' theatre presentations, comment mainly on the extent to which the performance reveals characters' emotions, motives, beliefs, and conflicts.

Useful Reference

Good-bye Round Robin contains useful information about readers' theatre as well as a range of possibilities for oral interpretation of literature.

Parameters for Effective Group Behavior

Some students do not work well in small groups. They are unfocused and unproductive. Interaction is often limited and one or two students seem to do most of the work.

Goal

To encourage students to work more productively and actively in small-group learning.

How to Reach It

Begin with 10–15 minutes of common-sense discussion about working effectively in small groups. Build a checklist of effective group behavior. Below is an example.

- Come prepared.
- Review the task before beginning work.
- Agree on roles. Who does what to complete the work?
- Invite all to participate and listen respectfully.
- Disagree without being disagreeable.
- Contribute relevant ideas.
- Contribute to the summary made after every group session.
- Responsibly complete assigned tasks.

Students could use the list they generated to complete self-assessments after each group meeting or task. Setting a personal goal for the next small-group experience should help each student to work more productively.

For students unfamiliar with or unskilled in group work, begin with short assignments and limited time frames. Clearly articulate the specific action required of the group work, for example, to agree on the three most important reasons for Confederation in Canada or to identify four possible motives for a character's behavior. Ensure that students review the task within the group, summarize their work at the end of the period, individually assess their own work, and state a personal goal for subsequent group work.

Begin with groups of two or three to nudge students to take active part in group work. Remind students that groups dissolve once a given task has been completed and re-form for different tasks. Students should work with different classmates for different projects.

Useful Reference

Cooperative Learning in the Classroom by David Johnson, Roger Johnson, and Edythe Holubec outlines cooperative learning strategies.

Student Assessment Form for Small-Group Work

Name _____ *Anika Phillips* _____

Assignment _____ *Character Study* _____

Due Date _____ *December 3* _____

Group Members _____ *Penny, Henry, Michael* _____

Please place a check mark beside each statement that accurately describes you.

CRITERIA

MY GOALS FOR FUTURE SMALL-GROUP WORK

✓ 1.   I came prepared to group meetings.

My goal is to stay on task and not waste time.

_____ 2.   I helped the group review the assignment.

✓ 3.   I helped the group assign responsibilities to complete the assignment.

_____ 4.   I helped the group stay focused on the assignment.

_____ 5.   I encouraged others to contribute.

_____ 6.   I stayed open-minded about different interpretations.

✓ 7.   I contributed to the summary and goal setting that concluded each meeting of the group.

Talking About Text

When it comes to talking about their likes and dislikes, your students are not shy. They are less enthusiastic, though, about reading text closely. While you seek to improve reading skills, you wish to focus on student-talk about enjoyable reading.

Goal

To encourage students to talk about favorite texts and to emphasize the personal value of reading for enjoyment.

How to Reach It

Invite students to reflect on all of the reading they have done over the past several weeks—both in class and elsewhere. Each student should choose a favorite section of text, possibly a third to a half of a page depending upon the format of the text. Students should then prepare competent oral readings of their excerpts. They should practise as much as they need to so that their presentations are fluent and expressive.

Have students work in small groups, where they can take turns reading their favorite sections. Before the reading, a student might offer background information to help listeners comprehend the text. Immediately after the reading, the reader should comment on why the text is interesting and enjoyable, then invite responses from the group. Listeners should share their own responses to the text, including questions and personal connections.

Discussing Thinking Strategies

Your students are comfortable working with partners to complete tasks. You decide to have them work in pairs with a text so that they can talk and learn about their thinking strategies.

Goal

To have students learn about personally effective thinking strategies through cooperative work.

How to Reach It

Select a text with which your students will work. As part of class discussion, decide whether students will read the text silently or orally with their partners. Specify three or four places where students will stop to discuss the text with their partners.

At each stopping point, ask the partners to take turns summarizing or paraphrasing what they read, predicting what follows, commenting about points of uncertainty, and describing personal experiences related to the text. For classes unfamiliar with the techniques, you will probably need to specify the thinking strategy that students should apply. Visualization, prediction, questioning, and monitoring-for-sense are among them.

After they have completely read the assigned text, have partners comment on important themes, emotions, and experiences suggested by the text. They should also comment on the thinking strategies that work best for them. (For example, they might say, "I pictured in my mind" or "I reread when I wasn't sure.") You could also prompt students to discuss how to improve their use of partner-reading on a future occasion.

Think-Pair-Share and Jigsaw Approaches

You are concerned about your students' ability to work cooperatively, especially since cooperative learning skills are emphasized in several curricula. You decide that a structured format would help your students improve in their ability to work in this way.

Goal

To employ structured approaches to improve students' ability to work cooperatively.

How to Reach It

A computer search of Web sites yields scores of pages about think-pair-share and jigsaw, two frequently employed structures to enhance cooperative learning. The following descriptions reflect personal preferences in use of the techniques.

Think-pair-share follows the pattern of individual reflection (think), working with a partner to refine understandings (pair), and then sharing with a group, often the whole class (share). Teachers often ask students to write down their ideas about the question or topic at all stages: to record what they thought originally, how their thoughts have been modified by work with a partner, and how their thoughts have been modified by group sharing.

The jigsaw technique derives its names from jigsaw puzzles is which each piece is required for a complete picture. Students in groups depend on other group members to complete a task pertaining to the topic. For example, if the topic is how characters are influenced by other characters, the teacher might identify five characters for analysis, one to be taken by each member of a group of five. The process involves three critical steps.

Step 1. Students are assigned to a jigsaw group to review the task and to review or negotiate the assignment of roles. At this stage, students could usefully ensure that they are clear about the task and about strategies for completing it.

Step 2. Students work with an expert group. For example, students would join other experts assigned to a specific character to discuss how that character was influenced by the other four characters.

Step 3. Students then return to their original jigsaw groups. Their shared task, using the example above, is to report on how *each* character was influenced by the other four. Each student teaches other group members about his or her specialty, but accepts contributions to refine interpretations.

Useful Reference

Cooperative Learning in the Classroom is recommended.

Part D   Viewing and Representing

Like speaking and listening skills, viewing and representing skills are receiving greater emphasis in program documents, textual resources, and classrooms. Educators increasingly recognize the importance of critical viewing and the value of representing to communicate meaning as well as to develop understanding. The word "representing" has been defined with variations in textual resources and program documents. In this book, representing refers to non-verbal communication, especially the creation of images and the use of gestures.

Viewing Media Critically

These activities focus students on thoughtful analysis of media.

- **Critical Television Viewing** (pages 104–5)
- **Word and Image in Advertisements** (page 106)

Focusing on Visual Images

These activities stress how the focus, lighting, color, setting, and characters of visual images convey meaning. When students attend to textual detail in their viewing and representing, their comprehension and communication skills benefit.

- **What to Do After the Lights Come On** (page 107)
- **Video Shooting Script** (pages 108–10)
- **Picturing Those Details of Text** (pages 111–12)
- **Figurative Language—It's in the Cartoons!** (pages 113–14)

Critical Television Viewing

You suspect that your junior high students spend hours per week watching television. You are concerned that they are not particularly critical in their viewing.

Goal

To motivate critical viewing skills through an analysis of familiar television genres.

How to Reach It

In preparing for the activity, you might remind students that by the time they finish high school, most of them will have spent more time in front of a television set than in classrooms. Remind them, too, that they will have witnessed thousands of violent acts and tens of thousands of commercials. With such exposure, students are wise to be critical viewers, especially of the values portrayed.

Remind students that a genre is a subdivision of a topic. For instance, stories, poems, non-fiction, and drama are genres of literature. Prominent television genres include soap operas, talk shows, situation comedies, science fiction, dramas, game shows, cartoons, crime melodramas, and advertisements. Every student or group will work with one genre.

Ask individuals or groups to analyze specific television genres suitable to their ages. They might use "Analysis of a Television Genre," the first page of which is shown on page 105. Photocopiable versions of both analysis pages appear as appendixes.

You will probably need to explain or review the term *jolt*. A jolt is an attention-grabbing moment of excitement generated by loud noise, rapid cuts (a sudden shift from one scene to another), a violent act, a quick movement, or a shocking image. Television critics have pointed out that without jolts, programmers would fail to command the attention of the audience. You may choose to model analysis by choosing one or two genres for whole-class work before you assign the genres for analysis by individuals or small groups.

Useful Reference

For de-constructing a variety of media, see *Media Literacy*, published by the Ontario Ministry of Education.

Analysis of a Television Genre

Genre ___SOAP OPERA___

Program Title ___"The Young and the Restless" episode___

SUBJECT(S)	IMAGE/CHARACTERS PORTRAYED	REAL-LIFE CONNECTION	EXPLANATION OF PORTRAYAL
The television program is about *several conflicts and conversations:* • *Jack/Nikki argue about a trip.* • *Jack/John argue about a trip.* • *Clyde worries about trial.* • *Blade and Neil argue about modeling contract.* • *Nathan and Olivia discuss house plans.*	The dominant pictures are • *well-dressed, rich people* • *attractive young people* • *business meetings* The feelings associated with the dominant pictures are • *positive feelings about wealth, power, success, being young and good-looking*	The television program is connected to real life in that • *lovers' quarrels are often portrayed* The television program is not connected to real life in that • *most viewers do not live life as it is portrayed. They aren't rich and powerful.*	The television program features its dominant images and characters so that the audience • *escapes to world of glamour* • *feels suspense (What happens next?) and keeps watching.*

Word and Image in Advertisements

Your students are often unenthusiastic when you try to teach them about literary technique. However, they are interested in television, film, and videos. You wonder if their interest in viewing activities can help them learn that authors of print, oral, and media texts deliberately employ techniques to communicate effectively.

Goal

To illustrate that communication techniques in advertisements are deliberate as are techniques used by authors of print text.

How to Reach It

Working with collections of magazines or videotaped commercials from television, challenge students to comment on the implicit message in advertisements and how words and images combine to imply the message. Remind students that messages or meanings are often emotional; the meaning may well convey a feeling about a product rather than an idea about it.

Note: Your work with this activity may serve to complement your attention to an author's use of techniques in writing.

The following sheet, shown in filled-in form, may usefully guide students' attention to word and image in advertisements. Students should select applicable questions from those listed under Images in the chart. The sheet can easily be adapted for work with videotaped advertisements. A photocopiable version appears as an appendix.

Useful Reference

For further information about advertising technique, see *Meet the Media* by Jack Livesley, Barrie McMahon, John Pungente, and Robyn Quin.

Word and Image in Advertisements

Advertisement   *Oasis Playa Hotel*

Source   *Vacation Catalogue*

Target Audience   *Young Travellers*

Time of Day (if applicable) _____

IMAGES	WORDS
• What is the focus?	• What message is conveyed by the words?
• Is lighting or color important?	• How do the words work with the images?
• What characters are used?	*Words such as "blissful" and "sparkling waters" suggest that the setting is beautiful and relaxing. This idea is also suggested by the picture.*
• What items are prominent?	
• What action is depicted?	
• What setting is employed?	
-young people enjoying beverages on a terrace by the sea	
-sunlight and blue sea and sky emphasized	
-a young man and woman are being served beverages by a friendly waiter	
-the couple is relaxed in the tropical setting	

EMOTIONAL MEANING	IDEAS SUGGESTED
• What feelings are conveyed or suggested?	• What ideas are conveyed or suggested?
relaxation, happiness	*The Oasis Playa Hotel is worth staying at.*

What to Do After the Lights Come On

You have shown a film such as Harry Potter and the Chamber of Secrets *to your class. As the credits come on the screen and you turn on the lights, students groan because they prefer the viewing to the ensuing discussion.*

Goal

To motivate students to appreciate the connection between technique and meaning in viewing activities.

How to Reach It

Help students attend to important details in the film or video just watched. First, ask them to note prominent images and sounds. This exploratory talk leads naturally to a consideration of reasons for emphasis on these details and to a consideration of meaning: the experiences, the emotions, and the ideas implied.

You may find the sheet "After the Lights Come On" useful for encouraging attention to detail as a prelude to thoughtful analysis of the film or video. A student sample appears below and there is a photocopiable version as an appendix.

Useful Reference

For further information about film study, see *Meet the Media*.

After the Lights Come On

Film/Video _____ *"Cosmic Zoom," National Film Board of Canada* _____

IMAGES
Indicate the images (pictures) that are emphasized in the film/video.
· *A boy fishing from a boat*
· *Camera zooms out to outerspace showing details of earth and beyond.*
· *Camera zooms back in to the boy towards an atom of a single cell.*

SOUNDS
Indicate the sounds that are emphasized in the film/video.
Music speeds up like tape on "fast forward" for zoom-out and zoom-in

EMOTIONAL MEANING
Indicate feelings conveyed by the film/video.
Respect for the complexity of the universe

IDEAS
Indicate ideas conveyed by the film/video.
The universe beyond us and within us is complex and beautiful.

Video Shooting Script

Many of your students watch television and movies frequently, but seldom read literature.

Goal

To motivate students to employ video techniques to read literature more thoughtfully.

How to Reach It

Review camera distance and camera movement techniques with the class. You may choose to use a film or video to help students learn about how film-makers use camera distance and camera movement to communicate meaning.

Camera Distance

- Long shot: a shot that includes most of the scene
- Medium shot: a shot that reveals a modest amount of detail
- Close-up: a shot that features a detailed view of an object or person
- Extreme close-up: a shot that features minute detail of an object or person

Camera Movement

- Cuts: rapid switches from one scene to another
- Pan: slow movement across a scene without interruption
- Zoom in: use of the zoom lens to present a closer view
- Zoom out: use of the zoom lens to present a more complete, less detailed view

After a class reading of "In Flanders Fields," distribute the video shooting script provided to illustrate how decisions about camera distance and camera movement combine with decisions about sound to communicate an interpretation of the text. Point out that the text of the poem is incorporated in the Audio section of the script and that numbers are used to indicate how audio and video work together in the presentation.

Ask students to select a poem, develop a video shooting script, and follow their script when filming. Let them work independently or in small groups. Once they present their videotapes, students might comment on their Audio and Video choices and how these choices related to the details of the text.

The rubric on page 110 may be useful in the assessment of videotaped interpretations of poems. Keep copies of excellent videotapes to serve as exemplars for future classes.

Useful Reference

Further information about filming technique can be found in *Media Literacy*.

VIDEO SHOOTING SCRIPT
FOR "IN FLANDERS FIELDS"

VIDEO	AUDIO
1. Long shot of military portion of cemetery.	1. Bugle or trumpet version of "The Last Post."
2. Close-up of Remembrance Day wreath with poppies.	2. Single Voice: "In Flanders fields the poppies blow Between the crosses row on row That mark our place;"
3. Long shot of birds flying.	3. Gunfire (from sound effects tape)
4. Close-up of a bird with zoom in to extreme close-up of bird's head.	4. Single Voice: "and in the sky The larks, still bravely singing, fly Scarce heard among the guns below."
5. Close-up of a headstone with zoom out to a few headstones.	5. Three Voices: "We are the Dead. Short days ago We lived, felt dawn, saw sunset glow, Loved and were loved . . ."
6. Blackout	6. Three Voices: "and now we lie In Flanders fields."
7. Long shot of traffic jam with cut to medium shot of children at play followed by close-up of one of the children.	7. Three Voices: "Take up our quarrel with the foe: To you from failing hands we throw The Torch; be yours to hold it high."
8. Long shot of four children standing in a semi-circle around a Remembrance Day wreath.	8. Three Voices: "If ye break faith with us who die We shall not sleep, though poppies grow In Flanders fields."
9. Blackout	9. Bugle or trumpet version of "The Last Post."

A Rubric for a Videotaped Interpretation of a Poem

	Level 4 Proficient	Level 3 Competent	Level 2 Novice	Level 1 Weak
PREPARATION	Demonstrates thoughtful preparation of shooting script.	Demonstrates acceptable preparation of shooting script.	Demonstrates limited preparation of shooting script.	Demonstrates little preparation of shooting script.
CAMERA DISTANCE	Consistently employs appropriate camera distance.	Usually employs acceptable camera distance.	Demonstrates limited attention to appropriate camera distance.	Demonstrates little attention to appropriate camera distance.
CAMERA MOVEMENT	Consistently employs appropriate camera movement.	Usually employs appropriate camera movement.	Demonstrates limited attention to appropriate camera movement.	Demonstrates little attention to appropriate camera movement.
AUDIO (VOICE)	Consistently employs appropriate volume, pace, and emphasis in voice.	Usually employs appropriate volume, pace, and emphasis in voice.	Inconsistently employs appropriate volume, pace, and emphasis in voice.	Seldom employs appropriate volume, pace, and emphasis in voice.
AUDIO (SOUND EFFECTS)	Consistently employs appropriate sound effects.	Usually employs appropriate sound effects.	Inconsistently employs appropriate sound effects.	Seldom employs appropriate sound effects.
MEANING	Consistently emphasizes an interpretation of the poem's thoughts and emotions.	Usually emphasizes an interpretation of the poem's thoughts and emotions.	Inconsistently emphasizes an interpretation of the poem's thoughts and emotions.	Demonstrates little attention to an interpretation of the poem's thoughts and emotions.

Picturing Those Details of Text

You harp on students using specific detail to support their interpretations of texts. While students are willing to offer opinions, they seem less enthusiastic about locating supportive details.

Goal

To encourage students to use representation to attend to the details of a print text.

How to Reach It

Activities that emphasize representation, that is, non-verbal communication, offer one method for students to attend to the details of text.

Recommendation 1: Challenge students to submit pictures that illustrate key moments or images from the text. The pictures may be drawn, clipped from magazines, or downloaded from image banks. When students present their collections, they should be prepared to explain why the pictures represent the text effectively.

The activity can be turned into a game if students develop collections of pictures for a variety of familiar texts. Classmates infer the title from the images presented. The images on page 112 point to *The Hobbit*.

Recommendation 2: A variation is to have students determine objects that would be in the backpack of one of the characters in a fictional work. These items can be listed or collected and presented to classmates. Consider having students collect artifacts for texts read by all or most students in the class since the beginning of the term, possibly anthology selections. Ask students to unpack someone else's backpack to infer the character and the title of the work and to assess the appropriateness of the artifacts. Another version of this activity is called the "artifacts box"; in this case, objects are packed in a shoebox.

Images from *The Hobbit*

Figurative Language—It's in the Cartoons!

You have tried to teach your students about figures of speech by having them find examples within poems being studied. Once again, you need toothpicks to keep your students' eyes open.

Goal

To help students learn about figurative language and other literary techniques through cartoons.

How to Reach It

Don't give up on having students identify figures of speech as well as other literary techniques in text. Encourage them to review cartoons and other popular visual communication forms to learn about figurative language and more.

You can use the following page to help students see how cartoonists sometimes employ figures of speech and other literary techniques, notably satire, to communicate. You can go beyond having students label techniques or figures of speech, such as similes. In addition to labelling, invite students to comment on cartoon meaning.

After students have learned about metaphor, pun, personification, irony, and satire through these cartoons, ask them to search the daily newspaper or cartoon Web sites for additional examples. They might record their observations in this way:

- Title of Cartoon
- Description of Cartoon (possibly with copy attached)
- Meaning Suggested by the Figurative Language

Finally, challenge students to re-visit print texts to consider the link between figurative language and meaning. They could record their thoughts in response journals.

"Figures of Speech and Satire in Cartoons," which features five numbered cartoons, illustrates the following techniques or figures of speech.

1. Satire: The ridicule of something to reform it. Example: *Mad* magazine satires of inferior movies.
2. Pun: A play on words in which the words are either identical or very similar in sound, but different in meaning. Example: A cemetery worker says that he is in a grave mood.
3. Metaphor: A figure of speech that involves an implied comparison between relatively unlike items. Example: "My brother is a bear when he wakes up in the morning."
4. Irony: One form of irony involves a contrast between what is expected or appropriate. Example: A thief discovers that his home has been robbed.
5. Personification: The representation of a thing or abstraction as a person. Example: "The moon smiled down on the young lovers." (Cartoon 5 also has puns.)

Figures of Speech and Satire in Cartoons

1.

2.

3.

4.

5.

Appendices

The following appendices are all photocopiable pages.

My Current Reading Profile

Create an accurate profile of yourself as a reader.

Date _____

The first part I look at in a book is

_____

_____

I like to read books that look as though

_____

_____

One thing that "puts me off" reading a book is

_____

_____

I usually read a book in about _____ (days, weeks)

My favorite authors are

_____

_____

When I describe myself as a reader, I usually use phrases such as

_____

_____

_____

My good reading habits are

_____

_____

_____

Reading habits I would like to change are

_____

_____

_____

My personal reading goals for this term (week/month) are

_____

_____

_____

Understanding Myself as a Reader

Title of Text _____

Strategies I used before reading:

Strategies I used during reading:

Strategies I used after reading:

My goals for future reading:

What I have learned about myself as a reader:

Unfolding Method Record Sheet

Title _____

1. ILLUSTRATION AND TITLE UNCOVERED, TEXT COVERED
   My background knowledge, predictions, and reading purpose:

2. FIRST CHUNK OF TEXT UNCOVERED
   My visualization, paraphrase, question, or prediction:

3. SECOND CHUNK OF TEXT UNCOVERED
   My visualization, paraphrase, question, or prediction:

4. THIRD CHUNK OF TEXT UNCOVERED
   My visualization, paraphrase, question, or prediction:

5. FOURTH CHUNK OF TEXT UNCOVERED
   My visualization, paraphrase, question, or prediction:

6. FIFTH CHUNK OF TEXT UNCOVERED
   My visualization, paraphrase, question, or prediction:

7. FINAL CHUNK OF TEXT UNCOVERED
   My interpretation, including answers to my questions and judgment about my predictions:

Reconsidering Interpretations

Title _____

After my first reading, I thought that

_____

_____

_____

_____

_____

Is my understanding as complete and accurate as possible?
As I went on reading, I came to understand

_____

_____

_____

_____

After carefully rereading the text, especially those sections that I wondered about, I now understand that

_____

_____

_____

_____

After discussing my understanding with others, I now think that

_____

_____

_____

_____

I am still not sure about

_____

_____

_____

_____

Cumulative Responses to Text

Title _____   Author _____

Once you have finished reading the book, write your response below. Feel free to respond to what classmates may have written about the book or respond to the book on your own terms. You might consider what you liked or disliked and why, what you wish had happened, what you thought of the characters, what the book reminded you of, how you reacted emotionally, and what questions you have about the book/novel. **Be sure to date and sign your response.**

A Wordsplash Sequence

I. TARGET WORDS

II. My predictions about the meanings of targeted words:

1. _____
2. _____
3. _____
4. _____
5. _____
6. _____

III. My understanding of word meanings from context:

1. _____
2. _____
3. _____
4. _____
5. _____
6. _____

Vocabulary Study

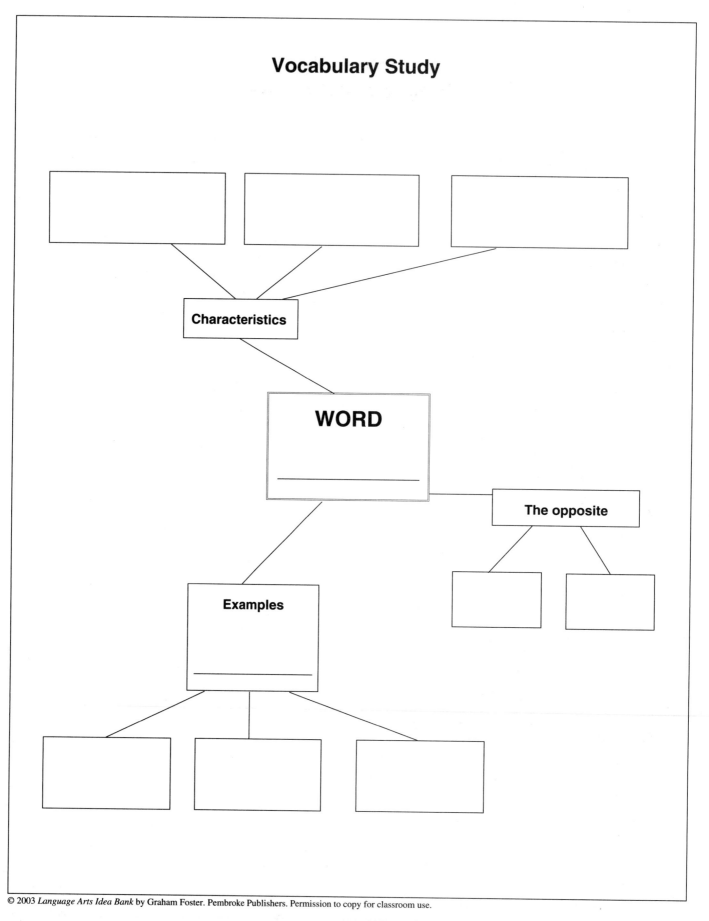

Characteristics

WORD

The opposite

Examples

To Be or Not to Be;
To Have and Have Not

Task: Identify at least five sentences that include any form of the verb "to be" and "to have." Rewrite the sentences to brighten these verbs.

1. Original:

   Revision:

2. Original:

   Revision:

3. Original:

   Revision:

4. Original:

   Revision:

5. Original:

   Revision:

Graphic Organizer for Web Searches

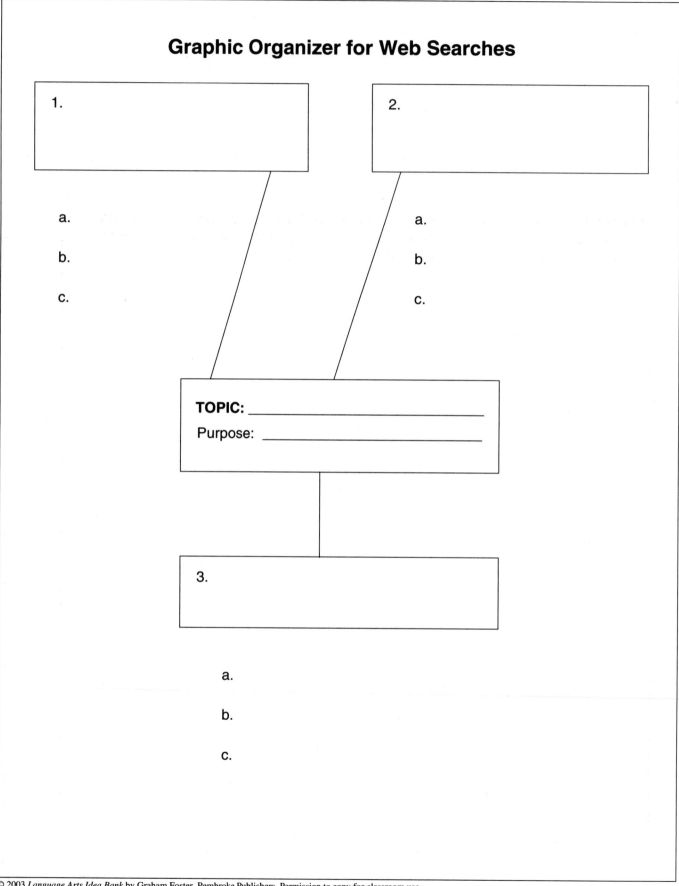

1.

a.

b.

c.

2.

a.

b.

c.

TOPIC: _____

Purpose: _____

3.

a.

b.

c.

How Do the Pros Do It?

I have this question about my own writing:

Below I have listed two or three texts that may help me answer my question.	Below I have written how the texts answer my question; there may also be an excerpt which helps me answer my question.

Understanding Myself as a Writer

Title of Text _____

Strategies I used before drafting:

Strategies I used during drafting:

Strategies that I employed after drafting:

My goals for future writing:

What I have learned about myself as a writer:

Learning Contract

Name _____ Class _____

TOPIC/GOALS

I agree to use the time allowed to work on the following challenge:

TIME ALLOWED

I agree to have the work completed by _____

RESOURCES

I will use the following print, Internet, media, and human resources to complete the project:

ASSESSMENT

My work will be assessed as follows:

Note: If a rubric has been agreed to, I will submit a self-assessment of my work with the rubric.

Assignment Completion Sequence

The Assignment _____

Important Requirements _____

_____

Due Date _____

Sequence

Date _____ | 1. |

Date _____ | 2. |

Date _____ | 3. |

Date _____ | 4. |

Date _____ | 5. |

Student Assessment Form for Small-Group Work

Name _____

Assignment _____

Due Date _____

Group Members _____

Please place a check mark beside each statement that accurately describes you.

CRITERIA   MY GOALS FOR FUTURE SMALL-GROUP WORK

_____ 1.   I came prepared to group meetings.

_____ 2.   I helped the group review the assignment.

_____ 3.   I helped the group assign responsibilities to complete the assignment.

_____ 4.   I helped the group stay focused on the assignment.

_____ 5.   I encouraged others to contribute.

_____ 6.   I stayed open-minded about different interpretations.

_____ 7.   I contributed to the summary and goal setting that concluded each meeting of the group.

Analysis of a Television Genre

Genre _____

Program Title _____

SUBJECT(S)	IMAGE/CHARACTERS PORTRAYED	REAL-LIFE CONNECTION	EXPLANATION OF PORTRAYAL
The television program is about	The dominant pictures are	The television program is connected to real life in that	The television program features its dominant images and characters so that the audience
	The feelings associated with the dominant pictures are	The television program is not connected to real life in that	

Analysis of a Television Genre (continued)

Genre _____

Program Title _____

JOLTS PER SEGMENT	VALUES SUGGESTED
In a segment of the program, the following jolts were employed:	The television program suggested that to be worthwhile, one should

Word and Image in Advertisements

Advertisement _____

Source (e.g., magazine, television, movie) _____

Target Audience _____

Time of Day (if applicable) _____

IMAGES	WORDS
• What is the focus? • Is lighting or color important? • What characters are used? • What items are prominent? • What action is depicted? • What setting is employed?	• What message is conveyed by the words? • How do the words work with the images?
EMOTIONAL MEANING • What feelings are conveyed or suggested?	**IDEAS SUGGESTED** • What ideas are conveyed or suggested?

After the Lights Come On

Film/Video _____

IMAGES

Indicate the images (pictures) that are emphasized in the film/video.

SOUNDS

Indicate the sounds that are emphasized in the film/video.

EMOTIONAL MEANING

Indicate the feelings conveyed by the film/video.

IDEAS

Indicate the ideas conveyed by the film/video.

Recommended Resources

Booth, David. 1992. *Stories to Read Aloud.* Markham, ON: Pembroke Publishers.

_____. 1996. *Literacy Techniques.* Markham, ON: Pembroke Publishers.

Carlson, G. Robert, and Anne Sherill. 1988. *Voices of Readers: How We Come to Love Books.* Urbana, IL: National Council of Teachers of English.

Caviglioli, Oliver, and Ian Harris. 2003. *Thinking Visually: Step-by-Step Exercises That Promote Visual, Auditory and Kinesthetic Learning.* Markham, ON: Pembroke Publishers.

Cook, Doris. 1989. *Strategic Learning in the Content Areas.* Madison, WS: Wisconsin Department of Education.

Foster, Graham. 1996. *Student Self-Assessment: A Powerful Process for Helping Students Revise Their Writing.* Markham, ON: Pembroke Publishers.

_____. 1998. *Standards for Learning: Clarifying Language Arts Outcomes and Helping Students Reach Them.* Markham, ON: Pembroke Publishers.

Foster, Graham, Evelyn Sawicki, Hyacinth Schaeffer, and Victor Zelinksi. 2002. *I Think, Therefore I Learn!* Markham, ON: Pembroke Publishers.

Hinson, Bess. 2000. *New Directions in Reading Instruction.* Rev. ed. Newark, DE: International Reading Association.

Hydrick, Janice. 1996. *A Parent's Guide to Literacy for the 21st Century.* Urbana, IL: National Council of Teachers of English.

Jobe, Ron, and Mary Dayton-Sakari. 1999. *Reluctant Readers: Connecting Students and Books for Successful Reading Experiences.* Markham, ON: Pembroke Publishers.

Johnson, David W., Roger T. Johnson, and Edythe Holubec. 1994. *Cooperative Learning in the Classroom.* Alexandria, VA: ASCD Publications.

Livesley, Jack, Barrie McMahon, John J. Pungente, and Robyn Quin. 1990. *Meet the Media.* Toronto: Globe/Modern Curriculum Press.

Macon, James, Diane Bewell, and Mary Ellen Vogt. 1991. *Responses to Literature, Grades K–8.* Newark, DE: International Reading Association.

McTeague, Frank. 1992. *Shared Reading in the Middle and High School Years.* Markham, ON: Pembroke Publishers.

Ontario Ministry of Education. 1989. *Media Literacy, Intermediate and Senior Divisions.* Toronto: Queen's Printer.

Opitz, Michael F., and Timothy V. Rasinksi. 1998. *Good-bye Round Robin.* Portsmouth, NH: Heinemann.

Scott, Ruth. 1991. *The Student Editor's Guide to Words.* Scarborough, ON: Gage.

Tsujimoto, Joseph I. 1998. *Teaching Poetry Writing to Adolescents.* Urbana, IL: National Council of Teachers of English.

Weber, Ken. 1987. *Precision Reading.* Markham, ON: Pembroke Publishers.

Winch, Gordon, and Gregory Blaxell. 1996. *The Grammar Handbook for Word-wise Kids.* Markham, ON: Pembroke Publishers.

Index